PREACHING
LUKE-ACTS

David Schnasa Jacobsen
and Günter Wasserberg

ABINGDON PRESS
Nashville

PREACHING LUKE-ACTS

Library of Congress Cataloging-in-Publication Data

Jacobsen, David Schnasa.
   Preaching Luke-Acts / David Schnasa Jacobsen and Günter Wasserberg.
   p. cm.
   Includes bibliographical references (p.) and indexes.
   ISBN 0-687-09972-2 (alk. paper)
   1. Bible. N.T. Luke—Homiletical use. 2. Bible. N.T. Acts—Homiletical use.
   I. Wasserberg, Günter. II. Title.

BS2589 J33 2001
226.4'077–dc21   00-068989

01 02 03 04 05 06 07 08 09 10 — 10 9 8 7 6 5 4 3 2 1

MANUFACTURED IN THE UNITED STATES OF AMERICA

To our wives,
Cindy and Solveig

CONTENTS

ACKNOWLEDGMENTS

Coauthors of a book are probably more aware than most that any writing is a truly corporate effort. Here we gratefully acknowledge the contribution of those people who have made this book better: the Reverend Cindy Schnasa Jacobsen, who patiently read more than one draft of some chapters; our colleague in New Testament at Waterloo Lutheran Seminary (WLS), Professor Tim Hegedus; Alannah Hegedus, who offered exceptional editorial help; Professor Bob Kelly; the Reverend Lynn Mitchell; the Reverend James Brown; the Reverend Gary Boratto; Professor Robert Brawley of McCormick Theological Seminary; and Professor Harold Remus of Wilfrid Laurier University (WLU).

The impetus for this book came at the end of Günter Wasserberg's visiting professorship at WLS in 1997–98. We had enjoyed working together so much during that year, we decided to put on a workshop at WLS for the benefit of our mutual friends and colleagues, the pastors of the Eastern Synod of the Evangelical Lutheran Church in Canada (ELCIC), as well as many ecumenical colleagues in the Kitchener-Waterloo area. The workshop, entitled "So That You May Know with Assurance: Lukan Narrative Theology for Preaching," was so well received, we decided shortly afterward to develop it into a book. Out of gratitude for their help and inspiration, we therefore wish to thank the many pastors who attended; Dr. Eduard Riegert for sharing his narrative preaching gifts that day; Pat Porterfield for all her help in arranging the workshop; our worship colleague, Dr. Donna Seamone, for her liturgical expertise as well as her encouragement; and, of course, the present and former bishops of the Eastern Synod, Michael Pryse and William D. Huras, for their unfailing support and interest in our efforts. All these people have in many ways inspired and moved us toward our goal.

The corporate nature of this work also extends to those either of us has worked with at WLS. Principal-Dean Richard Crossman, Professors Oz Cole-Arnal, Sarah Dille, Thomas St. James O'Connor, Peter VanKatwyk, Arnie Weigel, and the aforementioned Tim Hegedus and Bob Kelly have made WLS a wonderful place to teach and do research. We are grateful to them all.

Having expressed our gratitude in this way, however, we are also aware that the people above should not be held accountable for anything in this work that is less than satisfactory. Although they have all helped improve our work, it is doubtless our own intransigence that has resulted in any persisting errors.

The authors gratefully acknowledge that financial support for this research was received from a grant partly funded by Wilfrid Laurier University. The funds helped pay for the services of a gifted research assistant, Mona La Fosse, who aided us greatly in proofreading and in index assembly. Thanks also go to Professors Harold Remus of WLU and Paul Scott Wilson of Emmanuel College at the Toronto School of Theology, who helped us secure grant support for our research and writing.

Finally, it is important to acknowledge that some of the material you are about to read has first appeared elsewhere. The homiletical helps in chapter 1 were first published in *Word and Witness* ("Christmas 1," 94:1 [December 26, 1993], pp. 25-28) and later appeared in a bound volume of sermons from the same publisher, *Seasons of Preaching* (Eds. John Michael Rottman and Paul Scott Wilson. New Berlin, Wisc.: Liturgical Publications, 1996), pp. 53-54. The authors wish to thank Liturgical Publications for graciously agreeing to let us reprint the material here.

PREFACE FOR PREACHERS

In the middle of Luke-Acts there is an unusual conversation between two disciples on the way to Emmaus and, unbeknownst to those two, the risen Christ (Luke 24:13-35). In part, the two disciples have difficulty recognizing the identity of their conversation partner because of what they had recently witnessed, his grisly death on Golgotha the Friday before. The book you are reading now is similar in shape. It consists of a conversation between an exegete and a homiletician about the interpretation of the gospel in light of reading Luke-Acts as a single work, a consistent narrative. It gropes for the truth, yet does so in the face of the scandal of what happened—not just to Jesus, but to the Jewish people—through the so-called Christian centuries, culminating in the Holocaust, or *Shoah*.

Given such scandal, though, why choose Luke-Acts and not some other biblical writing? Many have recognized the centrality of Luke-Acts for the construction of the church-year lectionary used by many Christian denominations in the North American context.[1] Luke's annunciations and Magnificat have shaped our view of Advent; his Christmas story and account of Jesus' early childhood temple visits have been determinative for our worship in the season of Christmas; Luke's synagogue scene in Jesus' hometown has launched many an Epiphany; and, above all, his description of Jesus' postresurrection appearances and reports of early church life have left a distinctively Lukan imprint on the way we celebrate Easter, Ascension, and Pentecost.[2] In short, following the church year and the Revised Common Lectionary should require a generous footnote at the bottom of all our church bulletins and sermons giving Luke proper credit. The way we order our common worship life and preaching schedule is a tribute to Luke's narrative and theological genius.

Yet, as glorious as all this sounds, Luke's two-part work actually gives birth to a troubling liturgical and homiletical heritage. Luke, though an able storyteller, makes theological choices that are no longer fully open to us who live in the shadows of one of the bloodiest centuries in human history. Luke must find a way of explaining why the gospel is embraced by Gentiles but, for the most part, is rejected or ignored by the Jews. As our exegete will point out in subsequent chapters, Luke's answer is not just narrated with homespun stories, but explained theologically: Luke claims that *God* has hardened Jewish hearts.[3] In the face of this theological explanation many of us, with the horrors of the Holocaust still etched in our memories, can only moan prayerfully, "Lord, have mercy."

Our exegete, Günter Wasserberg, will help us understand historically why such a problematic theological move was made. He calls Luke-Acts, along with the rest of the New Testament (NT), a "grief document." This is to say, the varied responses of emergent Christian communities in the wider Jewish context are marked by grief over the fact that their Jewish contemporaries have not accepted and are not accepting the gospel that impelled Christians out into the streets of the first-century Greco-Roman world. I suspect that you will find, as I have, that Günter is an exceptional conversation partner as we try to come to terms with these and other aspects of Luke-Acts in our post-Holocaust context.

The primary method Günter uses in his interpretation of Luke-Acts in this book is narrative exegesis. Narrative critics ask questions of texts in ways quite different from others. Instead of assuming that the text exists to give objective data on historical personages, a narrative approach like Günter's interprets Jesus, Mary, Joseph, Paul, and Peter as characters in a story. The narrative exegete wishes to understand *why* Luke portrays these people as he does and how that affects us as readers. Similarly, rather than presuppose that Luke only wishes to mediate the events of history as they actually were, a narrative critic looks at *how* the events are related, or plotted, and what they are designed to evoke in readers. Yet because this book offers a narrative-*theological* approach, there is more here than simply an appreciation of literary art-for-art's-sake. Luke, Günter will argue, has a theological goal in portraying characters and telling the story the way he does: namely, to stabilize a mixed Jewish-Christian and Gentile-Christian congregation's identity in light of Paul's mission to the Gentiles.

Along the way, Günter's exegetical insights in the introduction and chapters 1-6 will call forth some homiletical reflection on my part in the form of "scenes." Why sermon helps in the form of "scenes" and not "points," "moves," or narrated stock "plots"?[4] Luke, we will argue, is a kind of pastoral, narrative theologian. He tells stories not only to evoke an experience of the gospel, as important as that is, but also to help his reader understand it theologically at the same time. By dividing the homiletical helps into scenes, we honor the narrative flow yet freely break out of that narrative world theologically in order to understand it in ours. Preachers who preach narratively will find the scenes of the homiletical helps section easy to incorporate into a narrative preaching strategy. Those who tend to think through a sermon text more theologically than narratively will also find that each scene has at its core a theological understanding. They should benefit homiletically, as well. Preachers should, at any rate, feel free to use or discard any such homiletical helps as needed. If the scenes provoke theological and homiletical reflection on the part of individual preachers of the gospel, they will have served their purpose. *Soli deo gloria.*

Nonetheless, the big question of this book remains: how will we deal homiletically with Günter's "grief document" reading of Luke-Acts in our Christian pulpits? As preachers and pastors, we must first admit that the grief continues. Our Christian inability to come to terms with our Jewish brothers and sisters plagues us to this day. What for Luke was a struggle within a broad religious tradition (the pluralistic Judaism of his day) has become a frequently bloody and abusive battle between two major world religions. In its wake are the events we Christians struggle not to forget: persecutions, pogroms, assimilations, and Auschwitz.

So what do we do? Proceeding "scene" by "scene" through

Luke-Acts, we begin perhaps with Luke's own gospel in a nut-shell: "repentance and forgiveness of sins" (Luke 24:47). To be sure, we cannot avoid the repentance required. If nothing else, Luke's universal scope of proclamation should not exempt us Christians! Yet the other side of the Lukan proclamation may prove no less difficult: "forgiveness of sins." Indeed, it is a hermeneutic of this gospel-in-a-nutshell statement that is at the heart of the problem—just who forgives whom and why? To engage critically Luke's two-part writing is not just an exegetical or even a homiletical enterprise, but a profoundly theological one. It goes to the core of how we understand not just Luke's Gospel (the writing), but Luke's gospel (his proclaimed theology). We have constructed our liturgical year and our preaching cycles around the gospel of a Gospel which, no less than any other part of the NT, has helped sponsor anti-Judaism among Christians and, much later, anti-Semitism.[5] To read Luke-Acts anew is to go to the heart of Christian worship and proclamation in the hopes that God can renew it.

So the issue may not be as we first imagined. Perhaps we ought not agree with Luke that the problem for the gospel is that God has "hardened" Jewish hearts. Maybe God actually wishes to soften ours, even ours, as this third millennium of the Common Era dawns. Then, after the humble conversation in the chapters that follow, we too may encounter the risen Christ only to find ourselves saying: "Did not our hearts burn within us while he talked to us on the road, while he opened to us the scriptures?" God willing, let it be so.

David Schnasa Jacobsen
Waterloo Lutheran Seminary (Ontario)
Christmas 2000

EXEGETICAL INTRODUCTION
TO LUKE-ACTS

Though it has been widely accepted that the Gospel of Luke and the book of Acts were written by the same author, whom we call Luke, it is nonetheless only recently that we have read Luke-Acts as one consistent narrative. Having discovered that we need to read both parts of the two-volume work in order to understand its meaning, it is surprising that people working on Luke-Acts often put only half of it under scrutiny.

This is, of course, largely due to the fact that the two volumes appear in different parts of the NT. Were the two not separated by John's Gospel, one probably would be accustomed to treating Luke and Acts as a single, consistent literary work. In fact, the only really convincing proof or hint to help identify the person we call Luke as the author of Luke-Acts is that "Luke" mentions a certain Theophilus as his sole addressee in the introductory remarks of both volumes—Luke 1:3 and Acts 1:1.

The real author of Luke-Acts never reveals himself. He is identified with the name Luke because the Pauline Epistles (Philem. 24) and deuteropauline writings (Col. 4:14; 2 Tim. 4:11) mention a certain Luke, a physician. Since the book of Acts largely deals with Paul, the church fathers concluded that this author must have been a companion of Paul. Moreover, because Luke-Acts conveys a great interest for socially and religiously marginalized people, which can be summarized in Jesus' saying that "the Son of Man came to seek out and to save the lost" (Luke 19:10), it was but one step further to identify this author with Luke, the physician. After all, wasn't this what doctors were there for—namely, to heal and look after those who were marginalized due to physical or mental illness?

The one and only direct clue to identify the author of Luke's Gospel with the author of Acts is that Theophilus is the prime addressee in both. The fact that the Greek text of the two volumes has never been found in one unit, but is always separated into two parts, is one of the reasons that NT scholars Richard I. Pervo and Mikeal C. Parsons have questioned the literary unity of Luke-Acts.[1] They come to the conclusion that the two works vary so much in content and style that, although they undoubtedly were written by the same author, they are nonetheless clearly different narratives with different emphases. Instead of using the term Luke-Acts, they suggest, we should rather speak of Luke and Acts. Granted, it is true that the two volumes vary in style and narrative strategies. But it is equally true that they are directed toward the same addressee. Only a change in addressee could prove that the two texts are totally separate literary units. To illustrate: imagine someone is writing an autobiography. There are parts in which the writer will rely on other people's information and comments, especially with regard to that writer's childhood; but when it comes to the writer's adult life experiences, it's a totally different picture. For that, the writer can rely on her own perceptions and insights and interpret them in light of her own experiences. So a writer would have to write almost two different stories about her life: one in which she relies basically on other people's information and one in which she uses her own interpretations. Yet the two are put together as one consistent autobiography. The two parts represent two sides of the same coin.

This is also true for Luke-Acts. The key theological theme remains the same throughout Luke and Acts. It can be summarized this way: out of the midst of Israel comes God's salvation for the entire world through Christ. This key theme is made clear in the very beginning of the Gospel of Luke when Simeon appears as a type character embodying the long-awaited hope for "the consolation of Israel" (Luke 2:25), which is actually the hope for resurrection (see chapter 1). This he foresees when he lays eyes on the baby boy Jesus. Along with the idea that Jesus is the fulfillment of *Israel's* hope is that he will also be the hope for the non-

Jewish world; in other words, universal salvation will be accomplished through Christ's (death and) resurrection (Luke 2:32). But we as readers have to wait for these prophetic announcements to be narrated as fulfilled. Whereas Israel is almost the sole center of Jesus' proclamation in Luke's Gospel, the Gentiles will become the focus in Acts. On this note, Luke ends the first part of his two-volume work (Luke 24:47; see chapter 3).

The Gospel ending is in itself sufficient, which means Luke's Gospel can be read as one literary unit, but it is obvious that we also have to read the book of Acts in order to get the fulfillment of the second half of Simeon's prophetic announcement, the inclusion of the Gentiles into God's covenant with Israel. Contrary to the traditional view of the Christian church, this inclusion does not happen in the (first) Pentecost story in Acts, which is a Pentecost for the Jews not only from Palestine, but also the (Mediterranean) world (Acts 2:5-11; see chapter 4). The Gentiles still have to wait until Peter meets Cornelius for their inclusion to be accomplished (see chapter 6). Therefore, the story of Peter and Cornelius can be labeled as the second Pentecost, the Pentecost for the Gentiles. In Acts 10, the theological program announced by Simeon in Luke 2 has been fulfilled for the first time. Luke's narrative could have ended here.

But it does not. For what reason? The answer is simple: because Paul's story has not been told yet. The second half of Acts is almost exclusively a story about Paul (see chapter 5 and conclusion). Peter, who has been the main character throughout the first half of Acts, steps back and gradually disappears after the last major breakthrough, the inclusion of the Gentiles, has been successfully accomplished in the Peter-Cornelius encounter in Acts 10. He obviously is not needed any longer, except for one thing: he will be the key defender of the Gentile mission at the apostolic council meeting at Jerusalem (Acts 15:7-11). This is surprising, because with the exception of the household of Cornelius, we do not learn of any further missionary efforts to Gentiles on Peter's part. Now Paul (with Barnabas) carries out the Gentile mission of the gospel, which again is somewhat odd, because the narrative focuses much more on Paul's missionary efforts to Jews than to Gentiles. The Lukan Paul always follows a certain pattern: first he preaches to

Jews, and then to Gentiles. He follows this pattern from the very beginning of his mission at Cyprus (Acts 13:5), and this then continues on in his missionary efforts at Athens (Acts 17:17), Corinth (Acts 18:4), and Ephesus (Acts 18:19). The Lukan Paul perceives himself basically as a Christian missionary to Jews. In this carefully structured missionary narrative, Gentiles are only included after Jews, and the proclamation of the gospel to them is, for the most part, a consequence of Jewish rejection (Acts 13:46; 18:6).

The Lukan Paul turns into a tragic figure. Although he behaves more like a Pharisaic Jew than one called to bring the gospel primarily to Gentiles (Acts 9:15), he is nonetheless chased and persecuted by the Jews. When he preaches in Lystra to a Gentile audience (Acts 14:8-18), he does not even mention Christ. Instead, he unsuccessfully attempts to convince his audience to turn from polytheism to monotheism—in other words, to turn away from idols to the God of Israel. Meanwhile, he behaves like a faithful Jew who wants Gentiles to become God-fearers, though "the Jews" are still after him, full of hatred, even coming from a different city to capture him and stone him (v. 19).

His miraculous survival is reminiscent of Jesus surviving the violent actions of the people of his hometown, Nazareth, in Luke 4 (see chapter 2). But, like Jesus, Paul will eventually succumb to Jewish attacks. Jesus' life ends on a cross, and Paul is arrested in the temple while he is practicing the Jewish rite of purification (Acts 21:26-28)! "The Jews from Asia" (v. 27) make false accusations against him. They even accuse him of behaving in an anti-Judaic manner: "This is the man who is teaching everyone everywhere against our people, our law, and this place [the temple]" (v. 28). We as readers know this for sure: Paul is innocent of all the charges against him. He has behaved in a much more Jewish fashion than would be expected from a Jewish point of view, and even more so from the perspective of a believer in Christ. Paul even violates the apostolic decree. Peter and James, who were the unquestioned authorities in the Christ-believing community at Jerusalem, had clearly decided that circumcision was no longer required (Acts 15:7-29). But what does Paul do? Having just left Jerusalem, he circumcises Timothy "because of the Jews" (Acts 16:3). The Lukan Paul turns out to be a staunch Jewish conservative, next to whom Peter and even James appear to represent the progressive, revolutionary force. Anybody who has some insight into the development of the early church knows it was just the other way around.

The faith in Christ that the Lukan Paul proclaims comes across as so utterly Jewish that even the Jewish king Agrippa is almost tempted to become a believer in Christ after having heard Paul make his case (Acts 26:28). The Roman governor Festus declares: "This man is doing nothing to deserve death or imprisonment" (v. 31). But since Paul had already appealed to Caesar, he cannot be released, but must go to Rome (v. 32).

Once he arrives there, he does not meet with believers in Christ—their role is limited to picking him up at the port of Puteoli (Acts 28:13-14)—but with the Jews of Rome. Again he claims in innocence that he has done "nothing against our people or the customs of our ancestors, yet I was arrested in Jerusalem and handed over to the Romans" (v. 17). Thus, it can only be called a tragic error that he was arrested and had to appeal to Caesar in order to save his life.

One last time, Paul attempts to convince his Jewish audience in Rome that Christ's kingdom is the fulfillment of Israel's long-awaited hope. But his Jewish audience reacts in a divided fashion: "Some were convinced by what he had said, while others refused to believe" (v. 24). This split reaction is not justified, for according to Luke, faith in Christ is in full congruence with Jewish hope and expectation. Negative Jewish reaction has been a constant throughout Paul's ministry. Consequently, he is now ready to draw an unavoidable, albeit painful, conclusion: *God* has hardened the hearts of most of Israel (Acts 28:26-27). Even though Luke downplays this same "hardening" in the parable of the sower (Luke 8:4-10)—contrary to Mark's version (Mark 4:1-12) and Matthew's adaptation in which he adds the quotation from Isaiah 6 (Matt. 13:1-17)—he gives special weight to this Hebrew Bible (HB) quotation by placing it at the end of his two-volume work.[2] The Lukan Paul has finally come to understand a divinely wrought correlation: Jewish rejection goes hand in hand with Gentile acceptance of the gospel of Christ (Acts 28:26-28). Paul will continue to preach the gospel to "all" (v. 30) who are willing to hear it, but it becomes clear that Jews have lost their privilege to be the first and prime addressees. Whoever fears—in other words, honors and worships—the God of Israel (the key criterion of a God-fearer; see chapter 6) and believes in Christ is welcomed, for "God shows no partiality. Rather, in every nation whoever fears him and acts uprightly is acceptable to him" (Acts 10:34, author's translation). The last chapter of Acts is the hermeneutical key to all of Luke-Acts. What bewilders us, as post-Holocaust readers, is that despite this view of Judaism and Jews who did not believe in Christ, Luke aimed to *strengthen* the faith of his audience. This is what he had set out to do in his prologue to Theophilus: "that you may know with assurance the truth" (Luke 1:4, author's translation). Thus, the ending of Acts has to be understood as the accomplishment of this task.

But how are we to deal with this narrative, and especially with its ending? The Christian faith, as Luke conveys it, does not merely have Jewish roots; rather, becoming a believer in Christ is viewed as the only legitimate way to remain truthful to Jewish faith and traditions. To do so, however, means nothing more and nothing less than giving up one's own Jewish identity. Even though Luke has a moderate stance on the Torah (see the apostolic decree), the salvific ground of a Torah-observant life is not only shaken, but replaced by a new foundation: faith in Christ. On this point Luke is exclusive. Tolerance in the modern sense of the word is alien to him, as it would have been to others at that time, Jews and Christians alike. This is where we have to distance ourselves from Luke without giving up our own faith. Faith in Christ must not mean denigrating Judaism. Both Jews and Christians, and for that matter Muslims, are right and wrong. Until the Messiah returns, we will have to leave the question open to God. Surely, we all will be surprised and amazed by the greatness and the grace of God.

CHAPTER ONE

The Presentation of Jesus
at the Temple
Luke 2:22-40

Lectionary: Year B, First Sunday After Christmas
Years A, B, and C, Presentation of the Lord

TEXT

²²When the time came for their purification according to the law of Moses, they brought him up to Jerusalem to present him to the Lord—²³as it is written in the law of the Lord, "Every (firstborn) male that opens the womb shall be called holy to the Lord"—²⁴and to offer a sacrifice according to what is said in the law of the Lord, "a pair of turtledoves or two young pigeons."

²⁵And behold there was a man in Jerusalem whose name was Simeon, and this man was righteous and devout, awaiting the consolation of Israel, and the Holy Spirit was upon him. ²⁶And it had been revealed to him by the Holy Spirit that he should not see death before he had seen the Lord's Christ [Anointed One of the Lord].

²⁷And inspired by the Spirit he came into the temple; and when the parents brought in the child Jesus, to do for him what is customary under the law, ²⁸he took him up in his arms and blessed God and said, ²⁹"Lord, now you let your servant depart in peace, according to your word; ³⁰for my eyes have seen your salvation ³¹which you have prepared in the presence of all peoples, ³²a light for revelation to the Gentiles and for the glory of your people Israel."

[33]And his father and his mother were astonished at what was being said about him. [34]And Simeon blessed them and said to Mary his mother, "Behold, this child is set for the fall and rise of many in Israel, and for a sign that is spoken against [35]—and a sword will pierce through your own soul too—so that the thoughts of the hearts of many will be revealed."

[36]And there was Anna, a prophetess, daughter of Phanuel, of the tribe of Asher; she was of great age, having lived with her husband seven years after her maiden age, [37]and as a widow until the age of eighty-four. She never left the temple, worshiping with fasting and praying night and day. [38]And at the very moment she came she gave thanks to God and spoke about him to all those who were awaiting the redemption of Jerusalem.

[39]And when they had completed everything according to the law of the Lord, they returned to Galilee, to their hometown Nazareth. [40]And the child grew and became strong, filled with wisdom, and God's grace [favor] was upon him.

(Author's translation)

INTRODUCTION

The presentation of the infant Jesus in the temple is programmatic for the entire narrative of Luke-Acts. If—as we have proposed in the Exegetical Introduction—Luke-Acts has to be read and understood from the end (Acts 28) to the beginning (Luke 1–2) and then reread from the beginning until the end in Acts 28, then the presentation story becomes crucial for an understanding of the whole. It provides the reader with some groundbreaking information about how to read Luke-Acts and what to expect from it.

In the concluding pericope in Rome (Acts 28), the Lukan Paul comes to understand that the Jewish rejection of the gospel and the turning to the Gentiles are divinely interrelated (vv. 25-28). That is simply how God operates: through Jewish rejection, the gospel goes out of Jerusalem (the aftermath of the stoning of Stephen in Acts 7 and 8) and eventually to the Gentiles (Cornelius and Peter in Acts 10 and 11).

The question this poses, though, is whether the turning to the

Gentiles is only an "accident" in God's saving plan. The Gentiles could be viewed as a second choice: if all the Jews—don't forget there are not only Jesus' disciples, with Peter in the lead, and Barnabas and Paul, but also thousands of Jews who were baptized and became Christians (Acts 2:41; 4:4; 21:20)—had successfully come to faith in Christ, then the gospel would not have spread to the Gentiles like it did. For Gentile Christians, the accusation of being a "second choice" after the Jewish rejection of the gospel could weaken their position and thus pose a major threat to the universality of Christian proclamation.

Therefore, Luke 2:22-40 becomes crucial. Its major point is to reassure the Gentiles of their place within God's people. Christian Gentiles play an intrinsic role in God's universal, salvific plan through Christ. Yet humanity's salvation comes from the midst of Israel. Christ is Israel's saving gift to the world. In and through him Israel is glorified. It is without question that the gospel is intended for the Jews, but *how* the gospel then actually reaches the Gentiles has to be seen in the course of the whole narrative of Luke-Acts. The Simeon oracle in Luke 2:33-35 will give some helpful insights as to how it will happen, portraying Jesus as a sign that will be spoken against (v. 34).

LUKE 2:22-40 IN THE LITERARY CONTEXT OF LUKE-ACTS

From the birth announcement and birth narrative stories the Lukan reader already knows that Jesus is the Son of God (Luke 1:32, "Son of the Most High"; Luke 1:35, "Son of God"). The primary focus of his life thus far in the narrative is to be Israel's "savior" (Luke 2:11). The term *laos*—"all the people" *(pas ho laos)*—in verse 10 is almost exclusively reserved in Luke-Acts for the faithful people of God, namely, Israel. Only in Acts 15:14 and 18:10 does it programmatically include Jews and Gentiles as God's "new" people in Christ. Interestingly, the term "savior" in Luke 2:11 comes before the titles *christos* and "Lord." Whereas Israelites and those who were familiar with Jewish customs and traditions (the so-called "God-fearers") also gave a political-messianic quality to the title *christos*, which is the Greek translation of the Hebrew *mashiach*, the way Luke uses it clearly refers to Jesus' death and resurrection. The hope of resurrection is called by Luke the hope of Israel (Acts 23:6; 24:15; 26:6-7; 28:20). It is the core of Luke's Gospel. There he differs from Paul's concept of the theology of the cross, although to call Luke's gospel a theology of glory (as Käsemann does) misses the point.[1] Despite the fact that Luke does not stress the salvific aspect of Jesus' death, he does put emphasis on Jesus' resurrection as Israel's (and thus also all humankind's) hope for eternal life. In this way, the cross is not an accident or a by-product but an intrinsic part of God's saving plan for the world.

Even though Mary has heard the good news about the holy child to whom she will give birth, the Son of God (Luke 1:32-35), she nonetheless sings to and praises God for her firstborn son in political-messianic terms (Luke 1:46-55). It shows that there is a difference in perception and understanding on her (Jewish) part. It will be interesting to see the further outcome of this tension.

A CLOSE READING OF THE NARRATIVE OF THE PRESENTATION OF JESUS AT THE TEMPLE

Mary and Joseph are portrayed as utterly faithful Jews. Eight days after the birth in Bethlehem, the infant Jesus is circumcised (Luke 2:21). What's so interesting about this is that Luke, whose narrative scholars have considered the most Gentile-oriented, is the only NT Gospel writer who records Jesus' circumcision. How much more would we expect this from Matthew! The Lukan Jesus is—as Jacob Jervell puts it—the circumcised Messiah.[2]

Mary and Joseph go up to Jerusalem to fulfill yet another Jewish rite, the purification of Mary and the presentation of their firstborn child. This incident must be seen in light of their keeping the Jewish rite of circumcision. Whether Luke actually gets the Jewish rites "right" may be a question for historians, but in the course of the Lukan narrative this episode shows the close adherence of Jesus' parents to Judaism. Using images and motifs and language full of allusions to Judaism, and beginning the narrative with Elizabeth and Zechariah, who is a priest in the temple of Jerusalem, Luke has yet to quote scripture. The first explicit scriptural quote, "as it is written in the law of the Lord," deals with the purification rite (v. 23)!

Luke thus seeks to demonstrate the Jewishness of Christianity, to show how deeply Christianity is rooted within Judaism. The Lukan use of scripture does not start with big theological issues such as the well-known paradigm of promise fulfillment, but with day-to-day, ordinary use. This certainly is not accidental, but is a careful narrative sign concerning how to read and thus understand Luke's presentation of the gospel. Luke does not so much demonstrate his skillful use—as many want us to believe with regard to the two introductory chapters, Luke 1 and 2—of Jewish (-Christian) tradition.[3] Instead, writing like a Greco-Roman historian with theological emphasis and great narrative skills, Luke deliberately and carefully leads his readers into a rural Jewish world. What Mary and Joseph do shows simply how faithful and devout Jews behave. There is nothing extraordinary and exciting about it; it's simply a description of Jewish life and custom.

Now take a look at Simeon. Luke portrays him as an aged man. He, like Mary and Joseph, is "righteous and devout" and is "awaiting the consolation of Israel" (v. 25). We get the impression that Simeon has been waiting all his life for *this* particular moment to happen. He has been waiting a long time to die, but he has been told by the Spirit that is holy—that is, by God—that he will have to wait to "depart in peace" (v. 29) until he actually sees and becomes a witness of the appearance of the Lord's Anointed One, the *christos*.

Here is good news for Simeon! His moment of consolation has come. He now sees the Messiah, the *christos*. And what a Messiah this is: a little baby. But as soon as Jesus' parents enter the temple, Simeon immediately knows that this is the moment for which he has been waiting. Now he can depart in peace. In this infant baby, "my eyes have seen your [God's] salvation" (v. 30). This story seems to be so irrational, yet it is beautiful. On the narrative level, Luke tells us that Simeon is a symbolic figure for the hope of Israel. Simeon represents Israel's longing and hope for consolation. Thus, one might guess that Israel would rejoice.

One thing is clear at this point: Jesus is Israel's long-awaited Messiah, a reality that will cause problems later. He is Israel's hope for consolation, which is not so much political-messianic as universal in scope. The Jewishness of this hope is made clear through the person of Simeon.

Yet listen to what Simeon has to say. This is surprising news for Jewish ears: God's salvation is not only for Jews but for Gentiles, too (v. 32). Although it's not yet clear how the Gentiles will be included in God's covenant, it is understood that they will play an intrinsic part in it from now on. This could mean that the Gentiles now at the end of times will march up to Zion as Second Isaiah envisions (Simeon's canticle, vv. 29-32, alludes to Isa. 40:5 and 49:6-9). But Luke does not actually quote Isaiah. We simply are not told yet *how* the Gentiles will be included; we will have to wait for the Cornelius-Peter story in Acts 10. However, that the Gentiles are a part of God's covenant is no longer a question.

What's interesting is that even though Luke is not explicitly quoting from Second Isaiah in Simeon's canticle, he will do so in the inaugural speech of John the Baptist (Luke 3:4-6). There we have a basis for comparing Luke's version with that of Mark and Matthew. In contrast with the other two synoptic Gospel writers, Luke adds one more verse to the Second Isaiah quotation that they both use. This verse therefore becomes crucial and must be viewed as programmatic: "And all flesh [that is, everybody] shall see the salvation of God" (v. 6). Luke adds the universalistic perspective of his Gospel. That is a striking difference when compared to the other two synoptic Gospel writers' use of the quotation. Before Jesus actually appears in public, Luke's readers are being reassured (cf. Luke 2:30-32) that he will be the universal salvific figure. Simeon already alludes to what John the Baptist will announce in public years later. The reader who then encounters the Baptist's proclamation can, in light of Simeon's words, be confident that Jesus is the universal savior—and according to scripture, too.

Luke also makes another thing clear: Israel is to rejoice in the fact that God's salvation through his son Jesus, the infant baby, will be extended to Gentiles as well. Salvation for all humankind comes from Israel's midst. What an honor and what a delight that Israelite parents give birth to universal salvation! This is how Luke 2:32 has to be interpreted. It does not matter whether verse 31 with the term "all peoples" (*pantes hoi laoi*) refers to all the nations, since it could also refer to Israel as the twelve tribes. Verse 32 makes it perfectly clear that the Gentiles are positively addressed by Luke's Simeon. God's salvation—meaning the hoped-for resurrection—is universal, and this hope has become a reality for Simeon in the infant Jesus. Out of the midst of Israel, Jesus is God's salvific gift to the world.

If this is clear, how then will Jesus' parents react? One could assume that, at the very least, Mary knows from the archangel Gabriel what a special child she has given birth to (God's son; Luke 1:31-35), but thus far she seems to dream, like many in Israel, that her son will free Israel from worldly—in other words, Roman—pressure and occupation (Luke 1:46-55). Does she understand what Simeon has just said?

The result of Simeon's canticle is that Jesus' parents begin to marvel (Luke 2:33). The Greek word *thaumazein* can mean "to wonder at" or "to be amazed." Yet it also carries the meaning "to be surprised," in the sense of "to be confused," "to be startled," or "to marvel." This last translation seems more accurate here; the word has the same meaning in Luke 4:22, in which the Nazarenes don't quite get it. They simply—as we will demonstrate in the next chapter on the Nazareth pericope—fail to see who Jesus really is, as Simeon has already foreseen. The Nazarenes are willing to see Jesus as a prophet, but not God's son. In Luke 2:33, a similar meaning of *thaumazein* is intended. Jesus' parents don't quite get the point.

Interestingly enough, Luke here refers to Mary and Joseph as Jesus' parents. This is a contradiction to what we as readers have already known since Luke 1. But this does not seem to bother Luke. He is not a modern author but an ancient theological historian. He has a premise and a specific theological drive. Since the divine origin of Jesus has been made clear right from the beginning, he can now go so far as to name Joseph as Jesus' father. But Jesus' true lineage will be reasserted when Luke introduces Jesus' genealogy in Luke 3:23, in which he refers to Joseph's fatherhood as a supposed one, that is, as a false assumption.

Even though both Mary and Joseph are mentioned with their reaction to what has been said about the infant Jesus, and even though both become the recipients of a blessing, only Mary is the addressee of the following oracle (Luke 2:34-35). Maybe this has something to do with the fact that soon Joseph will simply disappear from Luke's narrative scene and Mary will become the only earthly parental figure mentioned with regard to Jesus. At any rate, Simeon's oracle for Mary also has meaning for Luke's readers: now comes the news that the bright horizon the infant Jesus has opened up will also be overshadowed by conflict. This is the first time in the Lukan narrative that gloomy undertones are introduced. Up to this very point, everything seemed to be portrayed in bright, optimistic colors and joyful tones. The hope of and for Israel really had been given a brilliant and flamboyant start. Now the situation will change drastically.

Jesus, as Israel's hope for consolation, will be welcomed with joy, as one should expect. However, he will also meet with conflict and rejection, not accidentally, but as part of the divine plan: Jesus "is set for the fall and rise of many in Israel, and for a sign that is spoken against" (v. 34). The formulation "is set for" is grammatically a divine passive; in other words, *God* is the passively named author of the rejection that Jesus will have to face. This is an important note to the reader because it already puts the reaction to Jesus (in the Gospel) and to his apostles (in Acts) into a *theological* framework. Whatever else happens to the gospel news of salvation to all humankind, it will have to be interpreted in theological terms. It is no accident, then, that when the Lukan Paul summarizes in Acts 28 his (mostly) failed mission to Jews at the end of his journey in Rome, he does so in theological terms: "The Holy Spirit was right in saying to your ancestors through the prophet Isaiah, 'Go to this people and say, You will indeed listen, but never understand, and you will indeed look, but never perceive. For this people's *[laos]* heart has grown dull, and their ears are hard of hearing, and they have shut their eyes; so that they might not look with their eyes, and listen with their ears, and understand with their heart and turn—and I would heal them.' Let it be known to you then that this salvation of God has been sent to the Gentiles; they will listen [accept]" (vv. 25-28).

Luke starts his Gospel programmatically with an allusion to Isaiah (Isa. 40:5; 49:6-9 in Luke 2:30-32), includes a direct quotation from Isaiah in John the Baptist's sermon (Isa. 40:3-5 in Luke 3:4*b*-6), and ends his work with the well-known Isaiah quote about the hardening of Israel (Isa. 6:9-10 in Acts 28:26-27). It's also worth noting that in all three passages a term appears that Luke uses only here: God's salvation (*to soterion tou theou*, Luke 2:30 [the personal pronoun *sou* here refers to God]; Luke 3:6; Acts 28:28). This shows that Luke-Acts has to be read from end to beginning, and from beginning to end in order to be fully understood.

Another striking term Luke uses in 2:34 is *antilego*, "to speak against." Aside from this reference (the use in Luke 20:27 can be dismissed), Luke uses it to describe the Jewish rejection of the gospel message Paul has to face in Pisidian Antioch (Acts 13:45) and then in Rome (Acts 28:22). In other words, what Simeon announces comes to pass in the course of the narrative, particularly with regard to the figure of Paul and his "failed" mission to Jews. Jews are the ones who "speak against" the gospel. The proclamation to Gentiles only plays a minor role in the narrated events; Gentiles appear mostly in summaries (Acts 14:27; 15:12; 21:19) or are singled out in specific stories, such as that of Cornelius (Acts 10) or the Roman proconsul Sergius Paulus from Cyprus (Acts 13:6-12). The vast majority of conflict and rejection comes from Jews, as the Stephen story and Paul's mission efforts show. For even when the Lukan Paul in Lystra becomes less a Christian missionary than a Jewish one, in that he and Barnabas try to convince their Gentile audience to "turn from these worthless things [idols] to the living God" (Acts 14:15)—in other words, even when the two try to make God-fearers with respect for Judaism out of Gentiles—Jews from Antioch and Iconium are still after them and try to kill Paul by stoning (v. 19).

Does the term "the fall and rise of many in Israel" thus refer to these scenes in Acts in which Paul encounters Jewish resistance? If so, the words should be in a different order; first should come the rise (the successful mission of Peter in the first few chapters of Acts) and then the fall (the stoning of Stephen and Paul's failed mission to Jews). But if Luke has used the word order intentionally, then we have to look at the dynamic of falling and rising in the Lukan narrative.

There is a clear indication of what Luke has in mind when he has Simeon speak about the fall and rise of many in Israel. It refers to the people's reaction to Jesus in the course of the Passion story. Only Luke has the people side with the Jewish leaders and authorities in the course of the trial. If there was a clear distinction between the Jewish people and their leaders up to Jesus' imprisonment, this distinction disappears thereafter. When Pilate calls together the chief priests and the rulers and the people *(laos)*, announcing that he is about to release Jesus (Luke 23:13-16), they unanimously cry out, "Away with this fellow! Release Barabbas for us!" (v. 18), and "Crucify, crucify him!" (v. 21). *This* is the fall of the many in Israel.

But as soon as the crucifixion is over, the Jewish multitudes who are watching the scene begin beating their breasts as a first sign of repentance (Luke 23:48). And in the opening chapters of Acts, literally thousands of Jews are baptized (Acts 2:41; 4:4). Peter himself, even though he sharply accuses his Jewish hearers of responsibility in Jesus' death (Acts 2:23, 36: "Jesus whom you crucified"; 5:30), also knows why they did it: out of ignorance (Acts 3:17). In other words, if they had actually known whom they were killing, namely, the Son of God, they likely would not have done it. But this is how God operates; their crime, strangely enough, helped God's saving plan to be fulfilled. Part of this required that Christ should suffer (v. 18) before being resurrected (Acts 2:23-24).

The people who encounter Jesus will be forced to make up their minds about him. In reacting to Jesus, the "thoughts of the hearts of many will be revealed" (Luke 2:35). This is part of Jesus' mission. But it will also become clear that it's not simply a matter of human free will. For though God opens Lydia's heart toward Paul's gospel proclamation (Acts 16:14), God can also prohibit an openness toward Christ, as in Acts 28:26-27. It is up to God to open or close our hearts to God's salvific act in Christ. Whether we like it or not, this is how Luke sees it. He is trying to interpret Jewish rejection of the gospel. An answer such as "I don't know" is not on Luke's mind. God is the author of all things that happen. In this sense, Luke has a wholistic worldview. On the other hand, Luke does not make a philosophical statement about the human capacity to grasp an understanding of God; rather, he seems to be more concerned about the state of the community he addresses. Those who, in the light of Jewish rejection, struggle with their Jewish (-Christian) identity are precisely the ones Luke wants to help and stabilize. If Christ is *Israel*'s savior for all humankind, why is it that many Jews, or even most of them, reject this proclamation?

Even Mary will have to face this conflict about her son. The expression "and a sword will pierce through your own soul too"

(Luke 2:35) does not refer to Jesus' crucifixion, but to the idea that Mary also will have to make up her mind about her child. Her motherhood will not exclude her from the obligation to see in Jesus more than just her son or Israel's political redeemer. After all, Jesus is the Son of God! Thus, Jesus' real relatives are "those who hear [accept] the word of God and do it" (Luke 8:21).

The story about the prophetess Anna (Luke 2:36-38) functions as a link to Simeon's story. Just like Simeon, Anna is elderly. She spent her whole life at the temple. Anna symbolizes Israel's ancient faith. Whereas the "consolation of Israel" characterizes Simeon's faith and hope, Anna's hope for divine intervention is called "the redemption of Jerusalem" (v. 38). Again, it's an ambiguous expression. Certainly, it's not intended to contradict the content of Simeon's canticle, but it shows that even though Simeon has made it clear as to how this consolation has to be interpreted—as a universal hope—it will require much more education to be fully understood. This will be the function of the Emmaus pericope in Luke 24 and the opening Ascension scene in Acts 1: Jesus, the hope of Israel, is also the hope for all humankind. All who believe in him share the hope of their own resurrection.

HOMILETIC POSSIBILITIES FOR THE PRESENTATION OF JESUS IN THE TEMPLE

The narrative of the Simeon text, viewed theologically, is quite promising for the preacher. Examining Simeon and Anna within Luke-Acts as a whole, we need to think of how our sermon announcing Luke's universal Gospel might also emerge "from Israel's midst." A sermon that takes Luke's plotted theology seriously might embody the following narrative movement (indicated in bold words at the beginning of each scene).

Introduction

An introduction to this sermon might well begin by highlighting the conflict that drives Luke's narrative theology here. On the one hand, Jesus is welcomed into Simeon's arms and proclaimed with joy in Anna's voice. On the other hand, this same Jesus is announced through Simeon's prophecy as a "sign" of contradiction. A good sermon introduction should therefore open up the narrative problem by presenting some way in which Jesus is both celebrated and unexpected.

In Ambrogio Lorenzetti's painting *Presentation in the Temple*, all the major characters of the Simeon and Anna story are gathered at the altar. Mary and Joseph look on in amazed silence. The prophetess Anna fixes her eyes on the child. The bearded priest Simeon, with a look of great solemnity, stares at the baby in his arms. Yet the Christ Child in the center of the picture is surprising! Simeon, Anna, Mary, and Joseph are gazing awestruck at baby Jesus *sucking his thumb*. Well, "what child is this"? The family may marvel, the aged Simeon and Anna may prophesy and witness, but the little child—this thumb-sucking baby Jesus—he's not what was expected at all.

The conflict can be framed in the introduction with an image like this one. Now it should be possible to continue apace through Luke's theological plot.

Scene 1
Jesus' parents expect him to fulfill the law.

Here we begin to lay groundwork for developing narrative conflict. Our exegesis has shown that the Jewish piety of Jesus' parents is important in Luke's narrative theology. Therefore, we will highlight the same, noting how their ritual activity is connected to theological understanding. This opening scene might look something like the following.

We can surely understand Jesus' parents. They only expect their son to fulfill the law. Mary and Joseph are doing things by the book. Out of devotion to the law, Jesus' parents do ritual purification and go up to the temple to present baby Jesus along with the stipulated

sacrifice for poor parents: two small birds. Law-abiding parents like Mary and Joseph simply want their son to know the value of righteousness. Perhaps a little piety will rub off on the boy—call it family values. Jesus' parents expect him to do what any child of the covenant ought—that is, fulfill the law.

The point of this narrative development is to normalize this activity for contemporary hearers, to facilitate an identification consistent with Luke's narrative theology. In this case, we can simply use "updating" language to make theological sense of Mary and Joseph's plotted action so that contemporary hearers can connect with it. All the while, we are setting up the possibility of narrative conflict to follow. For though Mary and Joseph expect Jesus to fulfill the law . . .

Scene 2
Old Simeon in the temple reveals this baby
will fulfill prophets' dreams!

The issue set up here is a divergence of expectations. Mary and Joseph expect Jesus to fulfill the law—to be circumcised and grow up as a child of the covenant. Simeon, by contrast, sees even more in the child. In a scene of startling beauty, he welcomes the child into his arms and begins singing a song. This odd contrast of expectation and reality brings out the element of gospel surprise. Luke's narrative moves toward how the universal gospel's mission to the Gentiles will be fulfilled. Although that mission is only alluded to here, the beginning of that gospel surprise is welcomed in baby Jesus. Preachers would be wise to develop that surprise with a careful retelling of the narrative. Of course, an illustration couldn't hurt, either.

Simeon somehow discerns that baby Jesus is salvation incarnate. Imagine that! In the movie *Babette's Feast*, two elderly Danish sisters devote their energies to preserving the teachings of their late, pietistic minister father. They reluctantly take in Babette, a French woman who has had to flee Paris, as their maid. After winning the lottery, Babette expresses her gratitude by spending all the money on a sumptuous feast given at a gathering to which the sisters had invited disciples of their pietist father. As course after delectable course is served, the table conversation revolves solely around the late minister's teachings concerning disdain for the world and its pleasures—even as they obviously enjoy the meal. Yet one guest, an old, decorated military man, plainly revels in every delicious gourmet dish brought out. The others are less aware of the precious gift on the table, until the old officer finally blurts out what they have hardly realized: that a costly feast has been set before them all! Just like old Simeon, he has eyes to see the salvation before him.

With such narrative development, the preacher can set up a contrast of expectations. Yet scene 3 complicates the contrast further.

Scene 3
No wonder, then, that Jesus' parents marvel at the good news.

From the standpoint of Luke's plotted theology, we have discovered that Joseph and Mary are marveling, in the sense of being confused. They don't quite get the point. Consequently, for the sake of our sermon, we will develop their amazement in a way that represents a less-than-clear understanding of Jesus' significance—especially since we will learn in scene 4 that Jesus is destined to be a sign that is opposed. Again, using a kind of narrative updating, we can portray the scene to highlight this "confused" sense of Luke's theological interpretation of the holy parents' amazement. It might look something like the following.

Naturally, Jesus' parents marvel at the news. No doubt they must already be imagining the headlines back home: "LOCAL BOY MAKES GOOD" splashed right below the *Galilee Gazette*'s masthead. Or how about a banner headline across the top of the

Jerusalem Journal: "SOMETHING GOOD COMES OUT OF NAZARETH." Then there are the photos. A young boy with such prophetic promise will need to be pictured with all the bigwigs—high priests, teachers, and local government officials. And then, of course, there are the official parties. Such a long-awaited Messiah deserves the red carpet treatment. Oh, Joseph and Mary must be proud of their son—he's destined to fulfill all of Israel's hopes! Simeon's news about this little boy is indeed marvelous.

The style of this narrative development in the sermon is a little tongue-in-cheek. Just as this "marveling" represents the holy parents' sense of confusion at Simeon's good news, so also our depiction of it theologically plays up a kind of "success story" misunderstanding. Yet this narrative development in the sermon is not just for fun. It sets up a profound conflict as Simeon's prophecy continues.

Scene 4
But stop the presses: Simeon reveals
good news is bad news with Jesus.

Here the conflict comes to the surface. On one level, there is opposition to Jesus' person developed throughout the Lukan narrative, culminating in the cross. On another level, there is the broader struggle over the mission to the Gentiles. Luke's community would likely have known that such opposition was not only Jesus' experience, but also that of those who would carry out such a mission in his name. As such, this part of the sermon should not only continue to retell the narrative, but also weave into it experiences of opposition—or examples of disappointment in finding it—so that we can name those experiences theologically into our world as well. It might look something like this.

Apparently, the fulfillment of Israel's hopes and the Gentiles' salvation will bring opposition to Jesus. Can you imagine the holy parents' faces falling at the news? Perhaps Mary and Joseph should have seen it coming. Even the law can't guarantee parents that their children will grow up in the ways they expect. The "Dear Abby" column in the paper is full of letters about kids not turning out as hoped—even when their parents followed Dr. Spock's baby book to the letter! But what law-abiding father like Joseph wishes to have his son described as a "sign that will be opposed"? What kind of mother could be happy with a son whose life pierces her own soul like a sword? Apparently, there's a dark underside to Simeon's good news: the reality that Mary and Joseph's son will not be some rags-to-riches story of national triumph! Mary and Joseph may do things by the book, but in the temple, Simeon already sees a cruciform shadow cast across baby Jesus' face.

Preachers may be well advised to continue this opposition motif with further homiletical development. In fact, given the predilection of some to treat Luke's Gospel as a "theology of glory," it might be good to dwell on the motif anyway! Nonetheless, the reach of the bad news of opposition extends beyond the cross to include, later, Peter and Paul's struggles with what the mission to the Gentiles means. From a practical theological viewpoint, however, it also may invite us to reflect on where the gospel also engenders opposition today, especially when that universal gospel message (which includes even unclean Gentiles) is extended to those we deem unworthy or unclean. Preachers may wish to do their own illustrative theological naming at this point in the sermon.

Now we turn to the final homiletical scene. There are some for whom the bad news of opposition is good news after all!

Scene 5
Yet to people awaiting the good news, that's how salvation happens: the promise and the cross belong together.

With this final scene, we take up Anna's reaction to the events. We have noted earlier in the exegesis the rather odd notion that Anna should tell the good news after hearing the second half of

Simeon's prophecy. If it is indeed not intended to contradict his prophecy, we can narratively develop her proclamation in light of the seemingly bad news just shared. It might look something like the following.

For people expecting God's redemption, the promise and the cross go together. The prophetess Anna catches sight of this baby Jesus, this "sign of contradiction," and runs out into the street, even with Simeon's second prophecy still ringing in the air! Immediately, old Anna is set in motion, praising God and telling others about the child. Perhaps Anna has lived long enough to know that redemption and opposition—the promise and the cross, as it were—are of a piece. A church in South Dakota decorates its sanctuary in an unusual way every Lent. Like other churches, they set up a rough-hewn, wooden cross. But in order to get the cross to stand, they do more than simply lean it against the wall or suspend it from the ceiling. This congregation sets the rugged cross in a *Christmas tree stand*. Why? Perhaps they believe that the reality of the cross and the promise of Christmas belong together. Certainly, nothing but the hopes of Christmas can bear the weight of the cross. Now that's good news indeed!

Again, this part of the narrative would be aided by some more careful, theological development by the preacher. Pastors will wish to reflect on where the mission of the church to the world meets with opposition, even as it embodies good news. This programmatic story about Simeon and Anna is important for a similar reason. The universal mission of the gospel with regard to the Gentiles made it hard for Luke's community to cope with their mixed Jewish-Christian and Gentile-Christian reality. Perhaps gospel preachers need to discern where those same kinds of struggles are at work among us today.

CHAPTER TWO

Proclamation and Confrontation at Nazareth
Luke 4:14-30

Lectionary: Year C, Third Sunday After the Epiphany
Year C, Fourth Sunday After the Epiphany

TEXT

[14]And Jesus returned in the power of the Spirit into Galilee, and good rumors about him went out through all the surrounding country. [15]And he taught in their synagogues, being glorified by all.

[16]And he came to Nazareth, where he had been brought up; and he went into the synagogue, as his custom was, on the Sabbath day. And he stood up to read; [17]and there was given to him the book of the prophet Isaiah. He opened the book and found the place where it was written, [18]"The spirit of the Lord is upon me, because he has anointed me to preach good news to the poor. He has sent me to proclaim release to the captives and recovery of sight to the blind, to set at liberty those who are oppressed, [19]to proclaim the jubilee year of the Lord." [20]And he closed the book, and gave it back to the attendant, and sat down. And the eyes of all in the synagogue were fixed on him. [21]And he began to say to them, "Today this scripture has been fulfilled in your hearing."

[22]And all bore witness to him and marveled at the gracious

words that came out of his mouth. And they said, "Is not this Joseph's son?"

²³And he said to them, "Doubtless you will quote to me this proverb, 'Physician, heal yourself'; what we have heard you did at Capernaum, do here also in your own country." ²⁴And he said, "Truly, I say to you, no prophet is acceptable in his own country. ²⁵But in truth I say, there were many widows in Israel in the days of Elijah, when the heaven was shut up three years and six months, when there came a great famine over all the land; ²⁶and Elijah was sent to none of them, but only to Zarephath, in the land of Sidon, to a woman who was a widow. ²⁷And there were many lepers in Israel in the time of the prophet Elisha; and none of them was cleansed, but only Naaman the Syrian."

²⁸When they heard this, all in the synagogue were filled with wrath. ²⁹And they rose up and threw him out of the city, and led him to the brow of the hill on which their city was built, that they might throw him down headlong. ³⁰But passing through the midst of them he went away. (Author's translation)

INTRODUCTION

This passage is one of the most difficult and disturbing texts in all of Luke-Acts. The text is difficult because the passage doesn't seem to make much sense after a first reading. Why does the Lukan Jesus endanger and even "spoil" his first success after his impressive self-inauguration and gospel proclamation? After all, the first reaction of his hometown Nazarene audience appears to be positive (v. 22). What more could one expect from this "newcomer"? The Nazarenes seem to show interest in their native son. Evidently, they want to hear and learn more about him. Jesus seems to be picking up on their unspoken desires concerning his healing power, but strangely enough, he will refuse to do any of the things he apparently had done in Capernaum (v. 23). To put it bluntly, what's wrong with this guy?

Further, why does his hometown audience react so violently? They could just leave him alone—after all, he seems eccentric to them. What's even more startling is that they apparently want to kill him. In their eyes, he may be just one of those false prophets that rightly deserves to be disliked in Nazareth. So what's all the fuss about?

Well, it's not that simple, as we may have already guessed. The conflict between Jesus and his hometown is not a minor issue; rather, it has to do with Jesus' divine authority. The story clarifies how Jesus has to be viewed. This perspective is not negotiable. Naturally, we readers have the advantage of already knowing who Jesus is—namely, God's son (Luke 1:35; 3:22-38). But should not the good rumors about Jesus in all of Galilee (Luke 4:14) have included the notion of his divine sonship? We have good reason to presume that Jesus' hometown audience in particular would be open-minded and willing to take a positive stance toward a son from their midst. This conflict, however, is not to be prevented and it's vital for the course of the entire narrative.

LUKE 4:14-30 IN THE LITERARY CONTEXT OF LUKE-ACTS

All the important data for understanding Jesus has been presented and set on stage (cf. the previous chapter on Luke 2). The child Jesus has become an adult. He has been baptized under divine approval: "You are my Son, the Beloved; with you I am well pleased" (Luke 3:22). Now Jesus' identity is in the open. This fact is underlined by the genealogy that ends by restating Jesus' divine sonship (Luke 3:23-38). This genealogy differs from the Matthean version, which presents Jesus "only" as the son of David and Abraham (Matt. 1:1-17). Herein lies a great theological difference between the concept of Jesus outlined in Matthew and that in Luke. As we learned from the Simeon passage, the Lukan Jesus has a universal reach and outlook.

Jesus' divine authority has been tried by the devil. The temptation story in Luke 4:1-13 has to be understood as a first and last test of who Jesus really is. Jesus' successful handling of those tempting offers by the devil has rightly proven that he is God's son, the savior of the world. If this is clear, then the question arises as to how the *people* will react to him. What could be more obvious than to try his hometown people first? After all, they have known him for years—since he was a baby. He must feel close to them, and they to him. We would assume the people of Nazareth to be an ideal audience.

A CLOSE READING OF THE NARRATIVE OF THE PROCLAMATION AND CONFRONTATION AT NAZARETH

Although narrative analysis puts a different emphasis on looking at a text than source or tradition criticism, this time it's worth the effort to consider the text synoptically. Whereas Mark 6:1-6 and Matthew 13:54-58 have Jesus' unsuccessful proclamation in Nazareth as one of many stories of his ministry in Galilee, turning it into a rather minor incident in Jesus' journey (which will end dramatically in Jerusalem), Luke puts it at the beginning of Jesus' public ministry, and thus makes it very programmatic. Luke himself shapes this story, though he is also dependent on sources and traditions. One thing is certain: he has read and studied Mark's version. Paradoxically, the differences between the two stories hint at Mark as the key source for Luke. We can read Luke's Nazareth pericope as an interpretation and modification of Mark 6:1-6, as I'm going to demonstrate.

The opening verses, 4:14-15, function as both an introduction and a summary. They introduce Jesus' public ministry in Galilee and at the same time sum it up. After the successful defeat of the devil's attack on Jesus, it's now the Spirit who determines the dynamic of the narrative. Within a short span of time Jesus has already become a public figure, for "good rumors" (Greek: *pheme*) have spread throughout almost all of Galilee. Jesus' place to teach is the synagogue, but strangely enough, Luke refers to *"their* synagogues." Why this distancing from the synagogue? Has Luke picked up, rather uncritically, a habit from Mark's Gospel (1:23)? Or is Luke already hinting at the negative outcome not only of Jesus' teaching in Nazareth but of his entire ministry, which eventually will lead to his death on the Roman cross? At any rate, the reader gets a mixed message: the result of his teaching at "their synagogues" seems to be recognition and success, for he is "glorified by all." Is this a "double bind" message, indirectly criticizing the negative outcome of Jesus' efforts in Nazareth, or is Luke stating that glorifying Jesus doesn't necessarily presume a right understanding of who Jesus "really" is? In order to find out, let's make Nazareth the test case.

Luke portrays Jesus as being a faithful Jew. Brought up in Nazareth, Jesus regularly attends the synagogue service on the Sabbath day. This picture reminds us as readers of Luke's similar portrayal of Jesus' parents in Luke 2. But Jesus standing up to read from the Torah scroll does not necessarily imply a special sovereignty on Jesus' part. Instead, it tells us that Jesus behaves as a faithful Jew who accepts liturgical responsibilities. The scripture passage that he quotes is a conflation of two different passages from Isaiah 61:1-2 and 58:6 (in this order). This reversed order should not be overinterpreted to mean that the Lukan Jesus "reads what he wants." For that matter, we shouldn't expect the audience in Nazareth to have had Isaiah scrolls in their pockets to be certain Jesus is reading scripture in the right order. From a narrative standpoint, we just need to hear the synagogue lesson from the prophet Isaiah for this Sabbath. As a reader, that's what Jesus has presented—so far. The "I" is Isaiah's voice in Jesus' mouth. The words were good news for the people of Isaiah's time, and of course the question must arise as to whether and how they could apply to this present audience.

From a narrative point of view, verse 20 is key. This is indicated by the reaction of the Nazarene audience; Luke states that "the eyes of all in the synagogue were fixed on him." The room is filled with suspense. The audience seemingly acknowledges that Jesus is not just a typical synagogue reader—the good rumors about him must have spread to Nazareth as well. Thus, the key question will be *how* Jesus is going to interpret these prophetical words. The astonishing (and yet not astonishing) thing is that Jesus applies the words to himself. This does not come as a surprise to the Lukan reader. But how will the people of Nazareth react to this message? It's definitely gospel news. It must come as a long-awaited relief: good news for the poor, the release of the captives, the recovery of sight for the blind, liberty for the oppressed—in other words, a proclamation of the jubilee year of the Lord (cf.

Lev. 25:10). The biblical jubilee takes place every forty-nine years. Its arrival signifies divine intervention and results in social revolution. The jubilee year has as its main goal the establishment of a new social order, giving those who had lost out in the old system a new chance to recover. Whether or not their difficult circumstances were their own fault is irrelevant. The jubilee year of the Lord gives equal chances, a kind of new beginning, to all members of society.

However, whether this ideal was ever practiced is yet another question. We have good reason to believe it was more of a dream than a reality in ancient Israel. The jubilee motif has become very attractive in our time. The year 2000 was a jubilee year, not only for Roman Catholics but also Protestants and even nonreligious groups, who called for debt relief for impoverished countries. A jubilee year includes freedom from political, economic, and social oppression; at the same time, it is far more than just the introduction of a new social order. Jesus proclaims the beginning of an *eschatological* age, since it includes, for example, the recovery of sight for the blind. All diseases and ailments, be they physical, social or mental, are *now* to be healed. To say it with Simeon, the appearance of Jesus is the long-awaited time of the "consolation of Israel" (Luke 2:25).

So, how will the first public addressees in Israel react to this eschatological proclamation? This question cannot be answered if one follows only the first lectionary reading (Epiphany 3 C) because it ends with verse 21. From a homiletical point of view, this break in the text makes sense because it calls today's listeners to react, just as the Lukan text calls upon the Nazarenes to react to Jesus' prophetic announcement. But with respect to the second lection (Epiphany 4 C) from the Lukan Nazareth pericope, which is taken from 4:21-30, the textual division should be questioned. We need to know the first half of the pericope in order to understand the dynamics of the second half. However, since this narrative dynamic is difficult to deal with, those who divided it into two halves may have decided that a "torso" is easier to cope with than two parts that don't seem to make sense. Further, this passage seems to be an ideal text for source critics to examine, but even they have failed. As one of them, A. H. Leaney, wrote in his commentary, "It is not too much to say that Luke, in his desire to combine the narrative of a triumphant visit with a rejection, has given us an impossible story."[1]

But is it really an impossible story, or could it be that one needs to read the Lukan story as one consistent narrative in order to make sense out of the two supposedly disparate parts? I believe that the Nazareth pericope is an ideal prooftext for the validity of narrative criticism. Luke is not just a collector of different oral or written traditions that, if improperly put together, turn into "impossible stories"; instead, he is a skillful theological author who manages to incorporate oral and written traditions into a new story. Rather than accusing Luke of not being adept, we should follow the storyline as it is presented by Luke and attempt to make sense out of it. Thus read, the Nazareth pericope as a whole discloses a clear yet disturbing message.

The key verse is 4:22. One's understanding of this verse determines the overall interpretation of the passage. Jesus' self-proclamation puts the ball back into his audience's court. Now it's their turn to react. What do they think of this self-inauguration, his declaration that he has been anointed by God's Spirit to be the fulfillment of Isaiah's eschatological prophecy? Well, it's not so easy to discern the meaning of their reaction. Some scholarly debate has occurred over the Greek words *emarturoun auto*, in which *martureo* means "to witness." The problem has to do with the dative case *auto*. One possible rendering could be to understand it as a dative *incommodi*, in which case the word means "they witnessed against him." This makes it possible to come to a rather smooth understanding of Jesus' harsh reaction in the verses that follow. The conflict then lies in Jesus' self-proclamation. The audience is against this claim: they simply strongly disapprove. The NRSV has a different rendering. It translates *emarturoun auto* as "all spoke well of him." But this also could be misleading in that it gives an almost too positive undertone to the people's reaction. If we interpret the first part of the sentence positively, then we could be tempted to interpret *ethaumazon* in the second half as "they admired." However, it's more appropriate to give both parts a more neutral rendering. We should stick with the basic meaning of *emarturoun auto*, which is "they witnessed to him." Then *ethaumazein* should be translated as "they marveled" or "they wondered." The sentence then states plainly that his audience has become the witness of Jesus' self-proclamation, and that they have begun to wonder about it. How can this native son make this kind of claim? Thus they ask, "Is not this Joseph's son?"

These are the only words that are spoken by his audience during the entire story, but they are crucial. They will help to explain Jesus' ensuing harsh reaction. Again, in order to fully understand the implications of this rhetorical question, we need to remember how Jesus has been introduced by Luke. He is the Son of God (Luke 1:32-35). This pronouncement has been made public, receiving heavenly sanction at Jesus' baptism (Luke 3:22), so there can be no further doubt about who Jesus' father really is. The genealogy makes it clear from the outset that it is a false supposition to regard Joseph as Jesus' father (Luke 3:23). Of course, the genealogy then ends by stating that Jesus is in fact the Son of God (Luke 3:38).

Let's now return to the Nazareth pericope and look for further support for our thesis that these few remarks by Jesus' synagogue audience are crucial for the ensuing narrative. As mentioned above, Luke knows and draws heavily upon the Gospel of Mark while formulating his own story about the Nazareth incident. Mark takes the question of parenthood in a different direction when he has the audience ask about Jesus' origin as Mary's son (Mark 6:3). That Jesus is Mary's son is beyond any doubt; rather, it is his paternity that is under dispute. Thus, the question posed by the Lukan audience to Jesus is wrong from the very beginning. It proves that they have a false understanding of who he is. If this interpretation is correct, then it becomes clear why the narrative now becomes much more somber. It moves from good news to bad news, from salvation to judgment. In the end, there will be vigorous violence on the part of the Nazarenes. What a change of tone and temper! What a strange and uneasy story! Where is the gospel in all of this?

In order to comprehend Jesus' line of thought, we have to keep in mind that Jesus already realizes that his audience will not accept him for who he "really" is, the Son of God. This is crucial to understanding his argument, which runs as follows: *If you Nazarenes refuse to give me the honor I deserve, namely, to recognize me as the Son of God, then I will also refuse to do any signs and wonders in Nazareth.* From now on, Jesus is on the attack; his tone sharpens. Jesus is no longer trying to convince but to distance himself from the people of his hometown.

Foreseeing ("doubtless") that his audience expects him to do healing wonders, he quotes the ancient popular proverb, "Physician, heal yourself," which in this case takes on the meaning, "Heal us! Do wonders here as you have done in Capernaum!" Mentioning Capernaum at this point is odd since the report about him performing miracles there comes only *after* this story (Luke 4:31-37), which is yet another indication that Luke uses Mark's Gospel outline as his basic framework (Mark 1:21-28).

A closer look at Mark's version of the Nazareth incident is even more illuminating at this point. According to Mark, Jesus is anxious to do healing wonders, "deed[s] of power" (Mark 6:5), but, with a few exceptions, he is not allowed to do so. Thus, he retires from Nazareth with great disappointment, and "was amazed at [Greek: *ethaumazen*] their unbelief" (Mark 6:6). In the Lukan story, it's the audience that "marveled" (Greek: *ethaumazon*; Luke 4:22) at Jesus' teaching. The Lukan Jesus assumes that his audience is expecting healing wonders from him as a proof of his divine sonship, but he refuses to do them because, for him, the recognition of his divine sonship has to be acknowledged first. This presupposition is not necessarily valid elsewhere, but here in the Lukan Nazareth episode, it's a primary concern.

Comparing both stories, we could say that the Lukan synagogue audience is in the wrong "film." Expecting mighty works and healing wonders from Jesus, this audience would fit perfectly into the Markan story of Nazareth, because that's what the Markan Jesus wants to do: perform miracles. But the people are not interested. That's why the Markan Jesus leaves Nazareth disillusioned. The Lukan Jesus, however, seems to have "learned" from Mark's Gospel that one can accept wonders without belief in him, and that they don't automatically produce faith. The Lukan Jesus applies this bad experience to his audience and thus refuses to heal.

Moreover, the Lukan Jesus comes to the general conclusion that "*no* prophet is acceptable in his own country" (4:24, emphasis added). Again, a look into Mark's Gospel is quite helpful. Whereas

Mark describes Jesus' rejection in Nazareth as an exception ("Prophets are not without honor, *except* in their hometown, and among their own kin, and in their own house" [6:4, emphasis added]), Luke turns this exception into a general rule. The rejection is not accidental. It will be fatal for the people of Nazareth, for now Jesus will leave his hometown permanently. In preparation, he is going to use scripture to support his action. Both Elijah and Elisha were called to help non-Israelites in spite of a time of great need in Israel. The synagogue audience immediately seems to get the point. Jesus refuses to do mighty signs and works in Nazareth.

It would be wrong, though, to interpret these verses as a general refusal by Jesus to heal people in Israel. Only a few moments later, Jesus will be on his way to Capernaum. Israel remains his primary focus and Israelites his primary addressees. The hour of the Gentiles is yet to come. It is still, narratively speaking, a long way to the Cornelius story, in which the Gentiles will be given an opportunity to be God's holy people. Up to that point, Gentiles will still have to function as a kind of alternative audience who will receive the gospel if Israel refuses Jesus' offer of salvation. But what we can learn from the Nazareth pericope is that it foreshadows the rejection of Jesus by almost everyone in Israel during the Passion narrative. There the people will vigorously side with their leaders to have Pilate put Jesus to death (Luke 23:13-23). What a grim outlook! But this is how Luke tells his story about Jesus. It won't be the end, though, because immediately after the crucifixion, the same people who shout, "Crucify, crucify him!" are eager to repent and beat their breasts (Luke 23:48). Thousands of Jews will be baptized after Pentecost (Acts 2:41; 4:4). So Luke's narrative won't simply be an account of failure, but will also become a success story in terms of Israel coming to faith in Jesus.

Still, for now, the outcome in Nazareth is dismal. Jesus has hardly ended his words when his Nazarene audience fumes with anger. They expel him from the synagogue, drive him out of town, and prepare to kill him. That which had started out so promisingly turns into a life-threatening confrontation. His first narrated public appearance ends for the Lukan Jesus in an attempt to take his life. The sovereignty by which Jesus handles this threat to his life is not very consoling. The end of the story is difficult to take. It is in parts pure polemic. The account is not yet anti-Jewish, but, if misunderstood as a general remark about "the Jews," comes close to being so. One has to keep in mind, though, that Luke was writing his Gospel at a time when the synagogue communities and the kind of Christian congregations Luke addresses have split. This separation may have divided families and friends, who would now have become opponents. Separation usually leaves us with grief, an emotional state that is not always open to rational arguments. Instead, an emotional polemic can be a release for the pain.

These dynamics form the undertone of Luke's version of the Nazareth incident. We can be fairly certain that Jesus actually preached in his hometown. We can even assume from Mark's report that it was not a success. Yet the way Luke uses Mark's account and transforms it has to be understood in the terms outlined above. Luke turns the Nazareth incident into a confrontation story. Whereas the Markan Jesus leaves his hometown in silent disillusionment, the Lukan Jesus assumes an aggressive mood. Whoever denies Jesus' divine sonship is denied mighty works. There is no further attempt to help the people come to a more positive understanding of who Jesus is after their first and only remark, which becomes so crucial and fatal: "Is not this Joseph's son?" Sometimes a few words can have tremendous consequences. The Lukan Jesus seems to have learned from the Markan Jesus that miracles alone do not evoke faith. Trust in Jesus is the key to faith. This is the prosperous and productive side of the story. The other side of it has to be handled with great caution.

HOMILETIC POSSIBILITIES FOR THE PROCLAMATION AND CONFRONTATION AT NAZARETH

When we put the two lectionary pericopes together, we have a text that is truly troubling to preach. It seems to present a classic case of systemic dysfunction played out across Jesus' family and hometown connections. Yet even in trouble there is promise. My wife, a pastoral psychotherapist, is inclined to believe that greater insight is possible when such difficulty is encountered. "Move toward the resistance," she says out of her therapeutic wisdom. And so we will.

Scene 1
Jesus returns to Nazareth as the hometown hero.

Here we have the opportunity to set up a movement that will be key for this sermon. Scene 1 is about Jesus, the hometown hero. Yet we know his message will end up overturning that notion: he leaves as "the goat." The introduction should present the heroic notion of Jesus while also foreshadowing its reversal. It might go something like this:

There's a picture of a big welcome home parade after a war—one of those old photographs of soldiers coming home. Standing on the curb along the parade route are the gathered crowds. Some are smiling, others waving, still others hooting and hollering with delight and waving flags. But then your eyes move to look at the faces of the marchers as they parade down the street. They seem like the boys they were when they left, yet somehow the experience of war makes them look old beyond their years. Their eyes still sparkle, but look as if they've glimpsed death. They may be glad to be home, but their smiles seem more like smiles of relief than joy. Perhaps Jesus would understand. He returns to Nazareth flush from victory over Satan in the desert. His name recognition has soared since he now has such a good reputation as a healer and teacher. Yet while the hometown crowd welcomes him in style, something does not quite seem right. It may be odd, but try to picture it nonetheless: Jesus, fresh from the wilderness and more under the Spirit's power than his own. Picture this Jesus as the hometown hero returned.

With the idea established, we now turn to Jesus' first action in Nazareth.

Scene 2
He brings good news: he proclaims himself
the embodiment of their hopes.

This scene plays on two overlapping elements. First, Jesus demonstrates his piety by reading in the local synagogue. In this sense, he plays into their expectations: he reads a beloved scripture text promising salvation. The well-known healer is our local boy made good. Second, however, Jesus then takes those expectations to a new level by focusing the proclamation on himself: "Today this scripture has been fulfilled in your hearing." This scene will therefore need to embody the double-edged sword of its theology. Jesus does articulate the hopes and dreams of the hometown folk. Yet he doesn't stop there. He also connects those hopes and dreams intimately to himself. A preacher might try something like the following:

So what does Jesus do? He shows up for worship in Nazareth. He even stands up to read. The scripture text consists of some of the most soaring verses of Isaiah. Jesus, the local boy who made it big, reads a text so full of God's promises it makes every gathered Nazarene glow. By the end, the people are positively gushing. You know how it goes. Have you ever seen one of those services in which the children help lead worship? Everyone is dressed in his or her Sunday finest. Some of the younger children lead the adults in singing "Jesus Loves Me." Still later some of the youth get up to read, even if haltingly, the scriptures for the day. And then, to top it off, a recent graduate returns from college to give the sermon. You can almost imagine the worshipers saying to themselves, "Why, didn't he turn out well!" But now take the picture one step further. Imagine that college student standing up to preach and concluding the sermon with these words: "The promises of God are wonderful, aren't they? Well, here's the really good news. Now that I'm here, they are all set in motion. In me, all of God's promises are being fulfilled." This is essentially what Jesus says on the Sabbath day in Nazareth: "Today this scripture has been fulfilled in your hearing."

Now that we have set up both the expectations of the Nazarene community and Jesus' unique claims, it is easier to shift into our next scene.

Scene 3
Of course, such talk makes the locals wonder:
Is Joseph's boy up to the task?

Here the exegesis of the Greek might allow us to play on the dual meaning of "wonder" in English. As we have seen, the locals wonder over Jesus the faith healer. Now, however, given his claims that "this scripture is fulfilled in your hearing," they are also starting to wonder whether all this is true. "Is not this Joseph's son?" they ask. Here the narrative incorporates a key theological shift concerning the person of Jesus. We might develop the idea thus:

Suddenly, all talk of praise seems out of place. Jesus seems to have made a claim for himself that the locals in Nazareth are not yet ready to offer their "amen" to. "Isn't this Joseph's boy?" they wonder. And that is the issue, isn't it? Seeing Jesus in the flesh no doubt made it harder to buy into such lofty prophetic claims. Could they remember the boy Jesus playing in the street? Might they have seen young Jesus learning something of the building trade from Joseph? Or was it just that a flesh and blood person was standing before them in the synagogue that day? We don't know. At any rate, they could go no further with Jesus. They "wondered" about him. Of course, we may have a hard time understanding him, too. The Jesus in our minds walks ten feet off the ground. We are baffled by the fact that Jesus' own contemporaries don't seem to embrace him. Yet we must admit that there are times when we're not so sure about Jesus, either. Perhaps we "wonder" when we are broken, and Jesus doesn't heal us. Maybe we "wonder" when we are hurting, and Jesus doesn't heal us. Or perhaps we "wonder" when we are in deep pain, and Jesus still doesn't heal us. At moments like that, we may also be inclined to think of Jesus as did his Nazarene contemporaries: "A fine person, yes, with noble ideas—but isn't he Joseph's son?"

With this doubt raised, we now turn to Jesus' strange reaction.

Scene 4
Now Jesus refuses to deliver: no hometown healings in Nazareth.

This startling narrative element may be one of the hardest to pull off homiletically. It's not just that Jesus *can't* heal, it's that he *won't*. Underneath the narrative lurks an important theological notion. Jesus teaches that it is God's will *not* to heal the Nazarenes given their reaction to Jesus' eschatological self-proclamation. By not seeing Jesus for who he truly was, the eschatological jubilee has passed them by. Just as in the days of Elijah and Elisha, God has now extended his divine healing and promises to outsiders and foreigners. The danger here for the preacher is to overgeneralize. We have a rejection of Jesus by Nazarenes specifically, not by "the Jews" generally. It is far too easy for Christian preachers to mistakenly use this episode as a kind of type scene for a full-blown anti-Semitism. The key here may be identification. By identifying with the Nazarenes, we get at the underlying theological issue that is key for this text: the rejection of Jesus has to do with a false understanding of his identity. Is he "Joseph's son" or is he God's Son? When the latter is not recognized, Jesus will not heal, whether among Jews or Gentiles. We might negotiate such a tricky theological understanding this way:

Let's be honest: on the surface, the statement sounds implausible. Jesus refuses to heal? This doesn't seem to fit the Jesus we know. How could this be? We are tempted, aren't we, to assume there must just be some misunderstanding. We would love to find a reason to exonerate Jesus, to justify his position, but we can't. It's not that Jesus *can't* heal, he just flat-out *refuses* to heal the people of his hometown. It's not a misprint in our Bibles, it's not a mistranslation of the Greek, nor is it something we can write off in terms of cultural differences or the historical Jesus. As if to drive the point home further, Jesus chooses to illustrate his refusal by drawing on the Bible. "Just turn through your Bible," Jesus seems to say. "There's Elijah helping out a Sidonian widow, not folks like you. Go a little further, and check out God's track record through Elisha. Whom does he heal? Naaman the Syrian!" In short, Jesus is throwing the good book at the Nazarenes. It's not that he can't heal, it's that he just won't heal *them*—in fact, he will heal anyone but them!

Preachers may not need to spend too much time here. The idea, shocking as it is, has a tremendous force of its own. Yet by identifying ourselves with the Nazarenes, the narrative can continue to help us develop a theological understanding of where the text as a whole is heading. Were we to say, "Thank God that Jesus heals Gentiles like us," we would be forfeiting our opportunity to encounter Luke's narrative theology in all its homiletic impact.

Scene 5
So naturally the locals get angry:
the Nazarenes want to kill him.

By facilitating the identification with the Nazarenes, we can now move plausibly to this scene in which, of all things, Jesus' rejection meets our counterrejection. On one level, the issue is what happens in Nazareth that day—the crowd wants to kill him. But the scene also foreshadows another important moment: the crucifixion. Here, theologically and homiletically, our complicity in the narrative events becomes much more clear. Like it or not, to say that Christ was crucified is to indict not only nasty Nazarenes, jingoistic Jerusalemites, or even riled-up Romans. The crucifixion, like this attempt to kill Jesus in Nazareth, is a profound indictment of ourselves—our power games, our privileged religious systems, and our moneyed interests. If Jesus refuses to heal on our terms, we know there will be hell to pay.

> Perhaps by now we can begin to understand the crowd's actions. Sure, we have trouble seeing ourselves taking part in a bloodthirsty mob. We are reasonable people, pious people, and certainly not the kind of people who would put someone to death in a rage. Or are we? Truth be told, we religious folk are hardly exempt from such a charge. While we may not envision ourselves throwing an impudent prophet over a cliff, we do still live in a culture in which accounts are settled by means of deadly corporate action. Whether it's the fringe hate groups that usurp the power of judgment through domestic terrorism, or the death penalty, or even the state's use of assassination to pursue foreign policy interests (how many

times have we publicly discussed knocking off Castro, Saddam Hussein, or Milosevic?), we must confess that we actually still entertain the thought of solving problems this way. Given that, we suddenly can see what's going on in Nazareth. The people who were prepared to toss Jesus out of town and over a cliff look more familiar than we first thought. They are "us." No less than those who crucified Jesus and called for his blood in Jerusalem, we are part of the story.

There's a painting in Europe of the crucifixion scene. In the middle is Christ on the cross. He is just as we'd expect him—suffering unto death. Yet as our eyes circle around the cross, we see an unusual scene. All of a sudden we realize that behind the cross is not first-century Jerusalem, but a fifteenth-century European city. Around the crucified Jesus are portrayed not citizens of the ancient world, but people from the artist's own time. As we look at the picture, the truth suddenly dawns on us: those people who would kill Jesus— *they* could be *us*.

Placing ourselves in the narrative, we are now ready to be surprised by Jesus' sovereign grace in the scene that follows.

Scene 6
Yet Jesus passes through the crowd's anger as if passing from death to life.

Having laid the narrative-theological groundwork in scenes 1-5, we begin to arrive at Luke's theological thrust. If the attempt to kill Jesus also evokes the cross, Jesus' strange way of passing through the angry mob points proleptically to his resurrection. Preachers need not overemphasize this point; it will be enough to simply suggest its theological meaning. In the same way that the crucified Christ cannot be contained by our provincial sense of who deserves healing and when, so his resurrection is something that cannot be controlled. Just as the risen Jesus is "on the loose" despite the best attempts to control him, so also is this itinerant Jesus beyond the grasp of even angry crowds like ours.

Surely it was a strange sight. In the midst of an angry crowd, Jesus makes an odd exit: "passing through the midst of them he went away." We like to imagine grander exits, such as in shoot-'em-up movie scenes in which vengeance is delivered in bloodred technicolor or someone rides off into the sunset in heroic fashion. Yet Jesus did not operate by the crowd's moral compass to start with, nor does he begin doing so now. He just leaves. Then again, perhaps the picture is not as odd as we first thought. When Jesus leaves, he does so in a manner reminiscent of his resurrection. If the crowds, the religious authorities, and the Roman Empire thought to control Jesus by crucifying him, they were in for a rude surprise. This same Jesus would be resurrected. He was destined to be "on the loose." In the end, there is no point in trying to control or circumscribe his healing power. Like the same Spirit who led him into the desert and then out, this Jesus goes where he pleases. So he doesn't vindicate himself at the expense of the outraged locals; instead, he passes through them and leaves. After all, his jubilee of preaching good news to the poor, proclaiming release to the captives, declaring the recovery of sight to the blind, and setting at liberty those who are oppressed is just getting started. It will not be contained by the angriest of hometown crowds or even death itself.

Scene 7
Well, now it makes sense: Jesus is not just a homespun faith healer, he is the risen Son of God in whom we have faith.

With this scene, we now can make theological sense out of the strange events that have transpired in Jesus' hometown. The issue in the end is a christological one. A view that limits Jesus' anointed mission along racial, ethnic, or religious lines, or that denies his divinity, will fail. This view ends up as just one more box that is used to contain the universal power of Jesus' jubilee announcement. Jesus is not just a local boy become healer, he is infinitely more. We are not to have faith in "healing," but in Jesus as God's Son.

In taking Jesus for a hometown boy who had become a big name on the healing circuit, those who thought they knew him best (that means us, by the way) actually knew him least. Perhaps welcoming the jubilee kingdom requires all of us to give up what we are so sure we know: that might makes right, that my people are better than your people, that God loves only the right kind of folk, and so on. Indeed, by recognizing that Jesus is not just "Joseph's boy" but God's Son, we surrender our limited vision to a God whose strange, sovereign will is justice, healing, and mercy for everyone. Jesus' jubilee proclamation breaks the bounds of our parochial worlds, but it doesn't destroy them. For if we who live in our own hometowns don't recognize Jesus' universal mission—even to those people we don't like—we might not be healed, either. Why? Perhaps because when we fail to recognize his mission, we miss the most important thing of all: that we need healing, liberty, and good news precisely where we don't want it. Our vision of how we think God's Son, in his sovereign mercy, should heal us is too narrow. Maybe this is why Alcoholics Anonymous works so well. Not a few people have looked down on alcoholics; we have viewed them as bums, failures, or even worse. But it would be fruitless for the purpose of healing to focus on anyone's merit or ability to climb out of the morass that is alcoholism. Alcoholics Anonymous doesn't heal by asking alcoholics through some act of the will to believe in healing or even some wonder-working healer, but by inviting them to trust in a "higher power." Perhaps this is what Jesus' jubilee mission consists of: asking us not to rely on the strength of people like ourselves, but to trust in God's own son, Jesus, whose mercy is as wide as the world itself.

CHAPTER THREE

Hope for Resurrection:
A Learning Experience
Luke 24:13-49

Lectionary: Years A, B, and C, Easter Evening
Year A, Third Sunday of Easter
Year B, Third Sunday of Easter

TEXT

[13]And behold, that very day [Easter morning] two of them were going to a village named Emmaus, about seven miles away from Jerusalem, [14]and they were talking with each other about all these things that had happened. [15]While they were talking and discussing [debating?] together, Jesus himself drew near and went with them, [16]but their eyes were kept from recognizing him. [17]And he said to them, "What is this conversation that you are holding with each other as you walk?" And they stood still, looking sad. [18]Then one of them, named Cleopas, answered and said to him, "Are you the only visitor to Jerusalem who does not know the things that have happened there in these days?" [19]And he said to them, "What things?" And they said to him, "Concerning Jesus of Nazareth, who was a prophet mighty in deed and word before God and all the people, [20]and how our chief priests and rulers delivered him up to be condemned to death, and crucified him. [21]But we had hoped that he was the one to redeem Israel. Yes, and besides all this, it is now the third day since this happened.

[22]Moreover, some women of our company amazed us. They were at the tomb early in the morning [23]and did not find his body; and they came back saying that they had [even?] seen a vision of angels who said that he was alive. [24]Some of those who were with us went to the tomb, and found it just as the women had said; but him they did not see." [25]And he said to them, "O foolish men, and slow of heart to believe all that the prophets have spoken! [26]Was it not necessary that the Christ should suffer these things and enter into his glory?" [27]And beginning with Moses and all the prophets, he interpreted to them in all the scriptures the things concerning himself.

[28]So they drew near to the village to which they were going. He appeared to be going further, [29]but they constrained him, saying, "Stay with us, for it is toward evening and the day is now far spent." So he went in to stay with them. [30]When he was at table with them, he took the bread and blessed and broke it, and gave it to them. [31]And their eyes were opened and they recognized him; and he vanished out of their sight. [32]They said to each other, "Did not our hearts burn within us while he talked to us on the road, while he opened to us the scriptures?" [33]And they rose that same hour and returned to Jerusalem.

And they found the eleven gathered together and those who were with them, [34]who said, "The Lord has risen indeed, and has appeared to Simon!" [35]Then they [the two disciples returning from Emmaus] told what had happened on the road, and how he was known to them in the breaking of the bread. [36]As they were saying this, Jesus himself stood among them and said to them, "Peace be with you!" [37]But they were startled and frightened, supposing that they saw a spirit. [38]And he said to them, "Why are you troubled, and why do those [kinds of] thoughts rise in your hearts? [39]See my hands and my feet, that it is I myself. Handle me, and see; for a spirit has not flesh and bones as you see that I have." [40]Saying this, he showed them his hands and feet. [41]And while they still disbelieved for joy, and wondered, he said to them, "Have you anything here to eat?" [42]They gave him a piece of broiled fish, [43]and he took it and ate it before them. [44]Then he said to them, "These are my words that I spoke to you, while I was still with you, that everything written about me in the law of Moses and the prophets and the psalms must be fulfilled." [45]Then he opened their minds to understand the scriptures, [46]and said to them, "Thus it is written, that the Christ should suffer and on the third day rise from the dead, [47]and that repentance and forgiveness of sins should be preached in his name to all nations, beginning from Jerusalem. [48]You are witnesses of these things. [49]And behold, I send the promise of my father upon you; but stay in the city until you are clothed with power from on high." (Author's translation)

INTRODUCTION

The key function of Luke 24 is to teach the reader a lesson about the essentials of the Christian faith. As mentioned in chapter 1, the core of Luke's theology is the hope for resurrection that has been realized through Christ. Jesus Christ is seen as the fulfillment of Israel's long-awaited hope of resurrection. Yet this hope is not to be kept to Israel alone; it is to be shared with the entire human world. This hope for resurrection is Israel's fundamental contribution to the salvation of the world. Israel ought to be proud to have this universal savior come out of its midst. Jesus is not a revolutionary who invents a new faith, but a servant who carries out what Israel has hoped for throughout the ages. Thus, it is not accidental that Luke presents Jesus and his parents as faithful Jews—only Luke reports the circumcision of Jesus (Luke 2:21). Jesus is, as Jacob Jervell titles one of his essays, "the circumcised Messiah."[1] This is but one sign that demonstrates how deeply this universal Messiah, Jesus the Son of God, is rooted within Jewish faith and traditions.

With all this in mind, we might think that Israel would respond enthusiastically to the arrival of this long-awaited savior. However, even the faithful Jewish people *(laos)* eventually side with their leaders in the Passion story (Luke 23:13-18) and furiously shout out: "Crucify, crucify him!" (Luke 23:21). They have all become responsible for Jesus' death, but it is a tragic irony that through their participation in killing Jesus, they take on a necessary part in God's salvific plan, as Jesus himself has foretold (Luke 9:22; 17:25; 18:32-33).[2] But even his disciples did not comprehend what was to take place (Luke 9:44-45; 18:34). Thus, the question to be raised is: will they now at Easter understand that Jesus has risen from the dead?

DISAPPOINTED HOPE: TWO BEWILDERED DISCIPLES IN MOURNING ON THEIR WAY TO EMMAUS (LUKE 24:13-33*a*)

When the women who witness the empty tomb early Easter morning return and report what they have just seen, their words are evaluated as an "idle tale" by the apostles (Luke 24:1-11). The attitude is sexist: when women talk, they are not to be believed. So nothing has changed. It's the same old story again: Jesus is met with disbelief. Instead of joy and relief, there is mocking and skepticism. The routines of discipleship have regained control; life is back to normal. There's no further hope in Jesus. He's gone once and for all. This is the kind of mood Luke paints on Easter morning.

The two disciples who are on their way to Emmaus that same day share the despair of the others. We are not told why they are going to Emmaus. But it is obvious that they are not in a joyful mood. They are bewildered. They cannot understand what has happened to Jesus and thus to them. Jesus' death is to them an enigma, a riddle. They had "hoped that he was the one to redeem Israel" (v. 21). This hope has vanished after Jesus' death on the cross. This kind of death was not to be expected. Hope for Israel's redemption had a strong political side—many believed that Jesus would free Israel from Roman occupation. Mary sang the same song when she praised God for her divine pregnancy: "My soul magnifies the Lord, and my spirit rejoices in God my Savior. . . . He has brought down the powerful from their thrones, and lifted up the lowly" (Luke 1:46-47, 52). Zechariah sounded a similar note when he rejoiced over the birth of his son, John the Baptist: "Blessed be the Lord God of Israel, for he has looked favorably on his people and redeemed them. . . . that we would be saved from our enemies and from the hand of all who hate us" (Luke 1:68, 71). Who else but the Romans could he have meant?

For those who saw him as a political Messiah, Jesus was not supposed to die as a criminal on a Roman cross. Rather, he should have started a political revolution in Jerusalem. But, obviously, he failed and thus the high expectations regarding him must have been false. Jesus has left his followers and disciples in great disappointment. The walk to Emmaus can be described as a walk of mourners, not as a walk of people who have high expectations. This is strange, because up to this point nothing unexpected has happened. On the contrary, it has been said over and over again—mind you, by Jesus himself—that he must suffer and die and rise again on the third day (Luke 9:22; 17:25; 18:32-33). In fact, this was the third day. The women were at the tomb that morning and it was empty. And it was explained to them why it was empty and what this had to mean: that Christ had risen, indeed! The women remembered what Jesus had said, but are met with disbelief and mocking when they return to the apostles.

What do we as readers learn from this? It's obviously not sufficient just to be told that Christ is risen. It is more than just an intellectual enterprise. You have to have your own experience of Christ's resurrection. Moreover, without help from above there is no full comprehension of Christ's saving purpose. The two Emmaus disciples thus function as a kind of corporate critical reader. They raise the questions and doubts that the Lukan readers may have had with respect to Christ's resurrection. The dialogue about to begin between the two disciples and Jesus is a lesson in faith. Jesus appears as a teacher in matters of Christian essentials.

The dialogue is not without irony. The two disciples on their way to Emmaus have been blinded to Jesus' identity, yet they think that they have full intellectual insight and comprehension of what has happened. They try to teach Jesus a lesson about who he "really" is. In this they reveal no divine insight, but only their own foolishness (Luke 24:25), for they are wrapped up in their own frame of mind. They have no disclosure from on high. They are not open-minded at all, for their hearts—to use Lukan terminology—are locked and closed to the possibility of resurrection. Remember how Simeon once programmatically prophesied that one of the purposes of Christ is to reveal the thoughts of many hearts (Luke 2:35)? The Emmaus disciples should be embarrassed by their ignorance, yet they think that they know more about the situation and are thus in a position to criticize the stranger who suddenly accompanies them: "Are you the only visitor to Jerusalem who does not know the things that have happened there in these days?" (Luke 24:18). One is tempted to shout at these two disciples who think that they are bright, "Beware, don't you see that you are about to make fools out of yourselves!?" But it's too late; they are on the road to embarrassment.

The two Emmaus disciples tell their story in the only way they think it can be told, believing that they know everything that has happened. They present the simple facts, so to speak, that Jesus was a prophet mighty in deed and word before God, that he was crucified, and that it is now the third day since this happened. Still no bells ring. They continue to tell the story as they perceive it. "Oh yes, by the way, there are those women, you know, who went out to the tomb this morning and found it empty. They even had seen a vision of angels saying that he was alive—but him they did not see! So what else is there to tell? He's gone, you know, he's gone once and for all."

"O foolish men, and slow of heart. . . ." From our perspective, don't we think of these disciples in such a way? Yet Jesus is out not to destroy, but to build up, to help them gain understanding instead of embarrassing them. It may be that he even intends to draw the line concerning his identity once and for all, which he had done before with Jewish leaders—the Pharisees in particular—when he told them about the rich man and poor Lazarus (Luke 16:19-31). What a different Jesus there, it seems! He makes no attempt to convince or win the Pharisees for the Christian gospel. Rather, this story about the rich man and poor Lazarus is about final judgment, one that serves the purpose of distancing readers from "those Jews": "If they do not listen to Moses and the prophets, neither will they be convinced even if someone rises from the dead" (Luke 16:31). This "someone" has arrived and accomplished what "they" (the Pharisees and other Jewish leaders) will not allow themselves to believe in. Again, it's not a matter of pure intellectual insight, human effort, or capability, but of God's Spirit, which decides whether hearts are open to the gospel or closed. Thus, the seller of purple goods from the city of Thyatira, Lydia, a worshiper of the God of Israel, gains the ability to understand the Christian message only because "the Lord opened her heart to listen eagerly to what was said by Paul" (Acts 16:14). So it won't do to criticize the two Emmaus disciples for not having a better knowledge of Jesus. No amount of study was sufficient to open their hearts! As Jesus begins to interpret himself from the scriptures (Luke 24:27), they still don't get the message! They remain blinded by ignorance. Intellectual insight alone will not suffice. It requires disclosure from above.

"So they drew near to the village to which they were going" (Luke 24:28). Convincing someone who has become disillusioned that Christ is risen would seem to be a futile enterprise, but Jesus takes advantage of an opportunity when the two disciples invite him to join them. "You, stranger, do you have a place to stay? Why don't you join us for the night?" So he goes in to stay with them. The next part of the passage can be repeated word for word: "When he was at table with them, he took the bread and blessed and broke it, and gave it to them" (v. 30). Don't get too caught up with Christian doctrine here. It's not so much a question of whether this actually is Eucharist or not; Luke is vague on this point. What's crucial, though, is the combination of teaching and seeing. By itself, teaching about the resurrection is not sufficient. The Emmaus disciples need to see a proof—and they get it: the risen Christ himself! Jesus leaves the role of the disguised stranger and becomes the host of an evening meal, a (holy) supper. Breaking the bread means serving a neighbor. The roles have changed: the two men who think they are in control of the situation become the men whom Jesus serves. He's done this before. It's what his entire mission has been aiming at: to serve and not to be served or, in other words, "to seek out and to save the lost" (Luke 19:10).

Now the two begin to understand, for "their eyes were opened" (Luke 24:31). Again, understanding Jesus' identity is not a matter of human effort and insight; it requires help from above. Their eyes are opened, and now they are able to recognize him, and to remember. Now the scales fall from their eyes: "Did not our hearts burn within us while he talked to us on the road, while he opened to us the scriptures?" (v. 32). If this was the case, why didn't they recognize him before? Because they did not expect him to be at their side.

Once he is recognized, Jesus' physical presence is no longer required. Jesus vanishes and the two do not complain. There is no more mourning. Their hearts are now opened and thus they return to Jerusalem to proclaim Jesus' resurrection, just like the women who tried to do the same when they returned from the empty tomb. These disciples move from hope failed to new hope regained, not through human effort or insight, but rather through the risen Christ's breaking of the bread with them. Jesus has revealed himself as the hoped-for resurrection, as Israel's hope for redemption. The gospel is on the move. The disciples are eager to go back to Jerusalem and proclaim what they have just experienced!

A FINAL WORD FROM THE RISEN LORD: IT'S NOT OVER YET—THE GOSPEL WILL SPREAD FROM ISRAEL TO ALL NATIONS (LUKE 24:33*b*-49)

Back in Jerusalem, both groups have good news. Just as the two Emmaus disciples are about to tell what has happened to them, they learn from the eleven (Judas has left the scene and will appear once again for a final dramatic act of self-destruction in Acts 1:18-19) that "the Lord has risen indeed, and has appeared to Simon" (Luke 24:34). No longer just a rumor or an idle tale, now there is more proof: Jesus has appeared to Simon Peter. This reflects the earliest Easter tradition (cf. 1 Cor. 15:5), but here it's basically for the record, for we readers know that Jesus has already demonstrated in Emmaus that he is risen. The remark about Simon is not in conflict with the Emmaus story, though. Rather, on a literary basis, it serves to emphasize the importance and authority of Peter in the Lukan account, especially in Acts, and shows how central Jerusalem is for Luke. Whereas Matthew places the Easter appearances of Christ in Galilee (Matt. 28:7, 9, 16), Luke concentrates on Jesus' Easter experiences in Jerusalem. Jerusalem, with its temple, plays an important role in the Lukan concept of the history of the Christian gospel. Just as Luke opens his Gospel with a scene in Jerusalem concerning Zechariah's temple service (Luke 1:5-23), he also ends it in the temple of Jerusalem (Luke 24:52-53). Again, this is to show that the Lukan concept of Christianity is deeply rooted within Judaism.

With Luke 24, the Gospel story has reached its literary climax.

Since the Easter hope for resurrection is crucial to Luke's theological understanding, Luke 24 plays a very important part. After the first foundational "facts" about Easter have been narrated (Luke 24:1-11), the risen Christ appears and overcomes doubts about his identity. It takes quite an effort to convince the two Emmaus disciples, who recognize him only at the breaking of the bread. When they return to Jerusalem, it becomes obvious that other disciples feel a similar doubt. It's just not enough to be told that Christ is risen. You need to have your own Easter experience. The first reaction to the risen Christ is still bewilderment and fear, for the gathered disciples think they see a spirit when Christ suddenly stands among them (Luke 24:36-37). His words sound like a reproof: "Why are you troubled, and why do those [kinds of] thoughts rise in your hearts?" (v. 38). Although doubting Thomas (John 20:24-29) is not mentioned by name in the Lukan Easter narrative, this story would be perfect for him, because Luke reports a drastic and physical demonstration by the risen Christ that is unique and unheard of in all the other NT writings. Not only does the Lukan Jesus invite the disciples to touch him (as in John 20:27), he asks for food and eats a piece of broiled fish to show that the person in front of them is indeed Jesus, the risen Christ (Luke 24:41-42). Again, Jesus' attitude here is similar to the one he exhibited toward the two Emmaus disciples—which stands in sharp contrast to the story about the rich man and poor Lazarus that he told to distance himself from the Pharisees (Luke 16:19-31). Is there really much difference in attitude between the Pharisees he describes there and the disciples here? Not really, one must admit; but the Lukan Jesus relates to them differently. Whereas the story about the rich man and poor Lazarus functions as a literary device to distance the Lukan Christian community from the Jewish synagogue community and its (Pharisaic) leaders, this Easter demonstration aims to reassure Luke's community that the resurrection is a Christian essential. Different goals require different attitudes.

The following verses (Luke 24:44-49) contain the last spoken words of Jesus in Luke's Gospel. This gives them a special weight and meaning. In a literary work, final words function as a device to formulate a "last will." They are designed to leave an enduring impression upon the literary addressees and readers. Therefore, it is illuminating to compare Luke's Gospel ending with that of Matthew. The major difference is not in content, but in the structure of the Lukan narrative. Matthew's version ends with 28:20, but Luke's has a sequel, the book of Acts, and this second half is an intrinsic part of the entire literary work. As correct as it is to say that Luke's Gospel can stand on its own, we nonetheless should not forget that only in reading and studying both parts do we get the full panorama of Luke's narrative world. Luke 24 puts an end to the Gospel story, but it is an open or a preliminary ending. There are important events still to come.

With regard to Luke's theological program, which has been outlined in the Simeon sayings in Luke 2, one key prophecy, the inclusion of the Gentiles, still needs to be fulfilled. Thus far, they have been named only as candidates for the gospel in case Israel rejects Jesus and his proclamation (Luke 4:16-30). By no means are they only a second choice. Their time undoubtedly will come. Yet up to this point in the narrative, Luke has stressed the role of Israel as the prime addressee of the gospel.

Jesus reaffirms in his introductory remarks to the disciples in Luke 24:44 that nothing new has happened to him, at least nothing that should surprise them. Everything that has happened is in full accordance with what Jesus had announced before his death. To underline the fact that this is not something that Jesus has just made up, he adds that his fate is also in full accordance with *all* of scripture. Luke does not quote here from any specific HB book; rather, he stresses the general line of his argument that Jesus is the complete fulfillment of Israel's hope for salvation. What's interesting here is the term "Christ should suffer" (v. 46). Even though it's true that Luke puts a strong emphasis on the resurrection, it is nonetheless worth noting that only he uses the term "Christ should suffer" (*pathein ton christon*; Luke 24:26; cf. Acts 3:18; 17:3; 26:23). Only Luke uses the motif of a suffering Messiah, which is "not found in the OT or in any texts of pre-Christian Judaism," as biblical scholar Joseph A. Fitzmyer points out.[3] This shows that labeling Luke's theology a theology of glory is one-sided and false. For Luke, without an appropriate understanding of the cross there is no appropriate understanding of the resurrection. The cross is an intrinsic part of the gospel proclamation. Although Luke's theology is not a (Pauline) theology of the cross, to call it a theology of glory (Käsemann) is a false reduction that can only serve to disqualify Luke in comparison with Paul.

Another Lukan phrase here is striking, namely, that Christ's death and resurrection aim at "repentance and forgiveness of sins" (Luke 24:47). This shows also that Lukan anthropology operates with the notion of a humanity that has to be redeemed not so much in a political sense (see Luke 24:21), but in a spiritual sense through repentance and forgiveness of sins. In spite of criticisms that Luke lacks a soteriology here in Luke 24:47 (cf. Acts 13:38), it is present![4] Peter's Pentecost sermon can be summarized as a call to repentance (Acts 2:38). When Peter says that "whoever calls on the name of the Lord shall be saved" (Acts 2:21, author's translation), this is a soteriological statement.

What is new in these final words of the risen Christ before his ascension to heaven is the announcement that the time of the Gentiles is about to come. What has been announced in the Simeon canticles (Luke 2:29-32)—that the Gentiles will be included in Israel's promises—has not been fulfilled yet. The term "to all nations" (Greek: *eis panta ta ethne*; Luke 24:47) does not exclude Israel as the term *ethne* usually does. Luke and all the other NT writers are familiar with the traditions of biblical Greek, (i.e., the Septuagint), which distinguish between Israel and its faithful people *(laos)* and the Gentiles *(ta ethne)*. If "to all nations" in Luke 24:47 were to exclude Israel, the whole plot of the Lukan narrative would not make sense anymore, for in the beginning chapters of Acts, Luke still focuses on Israel as the prime and sole addressee of Peter's gospel proclamation in Acts 2 (see chapter 4). The Gentiles will still have to wait. Only when Peter encounters Cornelius does the gospel actually cross the boundary between Israel and the Gentile world. Yet what is important here is that the inclusion of the Gentiles is crucial to the final words of the risen Christ and represents his "last will and testament" while he is still on earth.

Jerusalem will be the starting point of this universal gospel proclamation. Beginning in Jerusalem, the good news will spread to "Judea and Samaria, and to the ends of the earth" (Acts 1:8). The time of the church is yet to come. The disciples are to "stay in the city, until you are clothed with power from on high" (Luke 24:49). Thus, these last words are no final commandment, but indicate an interim and show that Luke's narrative is not over, but awaits its continuation in Acts. The air in Jerusalem is filled with high expectation.

HOMILETIC POSSIBILITIES FOR HOPE FOR RESURRECTION: A LEARNING EXPERIENCE

Instead of trying to develop a sermon idea based on both texts, this sermon suggestion simply follows the Emmaus story while incorporating some of the important insights of the brief exchange in Luke 24:36-49. The purpose here is to take the narrative flow seriously, but to view its shape as having theological import for preaching.

Introduction

With the introduction we wish only to frame the story. The idea here is to set the scene and also provide a meaningful frame that will guide the development of the narrative to help it fulfill its theological intention.

> Preacher Fred Craddock says it well: "The longest trip a person takes is that from head to heart."[5] It sounds strange, but is often true. No doubt the disciples trudging toward Emmaus on the Sunday evening of the first Easter would understand. Oh, they've heard the good news, but they don't believe it yet. They are not ready to swallow such an unlikely tale. With vivid memories of Jesus' crucifixion still in their minds, they have a long journey ahead of them to Emmaus. In fact, they have one other journey that's even longer: the trip from head to heart.

Scene 1
The disciples on the way to Emmaus are disappointed with Jesus.

Here the preacher has an opportunity to enter into the narrative with power and poignancy. The scene begins with two disappointed disciples. Yet it might also end with preachers discussing such disappointment in our lives, as well.

We usually reserve for ourselves the pleasant fiction of contemporaneousness. If only we'd lived in Jesus' time, we could have enjoyed his presence. Had we been the innkeeper in Bethlehem, we would have found a room for the holy couple and child. Had we been at the crossroads, we would have understood why Jesus found it necessary to "set his face toward Jerusalem." Had we been at the first Easter, we would have welcomed the good news with pure faith and joyful hearts. Yet the disciples' reaction shouldn't surprise us. They are disappointed in Jesus. Their hopes had been dashed—mind you, not just because they refused to hear what Jesus said, but because they saw what happened to him. When you see evil seemingly triumph over good, disappointment is the only logical conclusion. The disciples knew of Jesus' death on the cross. They knew of its cruelty and its finality. That's why they walked to Emmaus disappointed. It's all they knew. It's all we might have known, too.

Scene 2
Jesus sees their disappointment and walks with them anyway.

Now, however, we begin to move into the strange mystery of God disclosed in Christ Jesus. Precisely in our disappointment, Christ walks with us, even if we fail to recognize him. As Luke portrays it, the encounter on the road to Emmaus is almost a humorous moment, to be sure, but it's also a profoundly gospel moment. Jesus walks with us in our disillusionment, loss, and in our ignorance, too! To make this claim allows us to become profoundly local in our pastoral theology. Here preachers may want not only to paint the unusual scene, but also to help hearers see disappointing places in their own life together where Jesus perhaps walks with them anyway. At this point, it may also help to continue portraying the Emmaus disciples sympathetically. We don't need to make them out to be intransigent or even comically thickheaded. The problem, if our exegete is right, is that the disciples are more "thickhearted." And we should understand that sometimes it is exceedingly hard to see what is before you when you are looking through tears.

Scene 3
Yet the disciples can't see him, because they can't see how the cross could ever help.

The theological shift here accompanies the shift in point of view from the previous scene. If Jesus' walking with them is something of a gospel moment, in this scene the disciples' inability to see the one who sees their disappointment has theological import. Our exegete notes that Jesus only reminds them of scriptures they had heard before. As such, the issue seems to be one of perception. Perhaps, then, they do not see Jesus because they do not expect to see a savior after witnessing the cross at Golgotha. In fact, it may just be precisely that experiential moment that makes the encounter with the risen Christ such a *non sequitur* for them.

Despite Jesus' presence on the road with them, the disciples fail to recognize him. Why? We aren't given much psychological information in the text to help us along the way. Nor do we have the benefit of much physical description. All we know is that the same disciples who saw Jesus killed on the cross were not now expecting to run into him at home, at the city gate, or much less on some godforsaken road. In other words, seeing Jesus crucified must have left them a little theologically cross-eyed. And should we be surprised? The last person we'd expect to bring salvation would be someone who was mocked and killed three days earlier. The humiliation and the sheer starkness of such a death would be too fresh in our minds.

We would never expect to see the object of our loss walking along the road. The disciples don't expect to see Jesus because that's not how saviors rescue, nor is it how crucifixion stories end.

Scene 4
So the disciples decide to show pity on the stranger by inviting him to dinner.

Although the scene has comic undertones, the disciples are not buffoons. It is not surprising that, shortly after the shock and dis-illusionment of the cross, they should find it difficult to see Jesus for who he is. At this point, the crucified Christ is little more than an object of pity for them. If so, is it not natural that they should treat this mysterious stranger traveling with them in an analogous way? What we have is a classic scene in which a misunderstanding, a misrecognition, escalates into an action that only lifts the irony to new heights. Since mistaken identity is such a frequent occurrence in literature and drama (the story of Jacob and Esau, *The Importance of Being Earnest*), the preacher has ample examples with which to sweeten such dramatic tension and exemplify it for the hearers.

Scene 5
Yet Jesus turns the tables on his guests by acting as the host.

Now the narrative takes a most interesting theological turn. The stranger, though invited to a meal, seems to break protocol. Rather than being served, he does some serving himself. Again, preachers have a marvelous opportunity. Here we may just wish to stay with the narrative and draw the picture with a kind of playfulness.

So what does the disciples' charity project do? Why, he takes the bread, blesses it, breaks it, and gives it to them. This was unheard of! Yet this guest seems determined to act as the host and serve the ones who invited him in the first place. Oh sure, we think we have

heard about these types before—the party guests who are just a little too eager. They're the first to clear the table, to wash the dishes,
or maybe even to take it upon themselves to clean up after all the
other guests have left. But this episode on the road to Emmaus
does all those experiences one better. Here, this stranger assumes
the role of host, not after the dinner's over, but to get the party
rolling from the beginning! By breaking the bread, the stranger
announces that he is the one who will serve them from this point
forward.

Scene 6
Now they finally get the picture: this sorry stranger
is Jesus himself, risen from the dead.

Now we shift from Jesus' action to the disciples' recognition of
him. It is precisely in his role as host that they realize who he is.
Think about how often you see someone out of context, such as a
colleague who works on another floor at the office. When you
encounter her outside of work, you scratch your head and try hard
to remember who she is. But it's nearly impossible unless you see
her do something she also does at the office. All of a sudden, the
resurrection truth dawns on the disciples. Not, mind you, because
there is a sudden manifestation of his divinity, but because, of all
things, he serves. Now that's him! That's Jesus! Imagine that—he
is risen, indeed!

Scene 7
So now they return home to proclaim the good news
even in the dark of night.

Now, thanks to their encounter with Jesus, the Emmaus disciples have glimpsed a new worldview that turns them around 180
degrees. So the disciples go the opposite way. The text says rather
blandly that they "returned to Jerusalem," which gives the impression that it was an ordinary journey. Yet please note: they return to
Jerusalem *after a full day of trudging in the opposite direction.* What is

more, they don't hurry back with the benefit of a good night's rest. The text says they arose (from a state as good as death, no doubt) that same hour. They were ready to run and proclaim the news *in the middle of the dark night.*[6]

The "young cities" of Lima are not the places most tourists tend to visit in Peru. They are places of poverty and struggle. Most people prefer to head to the great Inca sites in the south: Machu Picchu and other memorials to past greatness. Even if one were to venture to some of the poorer parts of greater Lima, few would think of going to one of the "young cities" at night.

But what do you do if you, as a visitor, wish to be with your brothers and sisters in Christ on the Lord's day? Well, first you have to stop thinking like a North American Christian. Most people in Peru don't work neat nine-to-five jobs. They also don't tend to take a day off. So on Sunday, if you want to worship with other Christians in the Two-Thirds World, there's a good chance you'll need to worship on Sunday night. But what a sight it is. To worship God in the gathering darkness is itself a proclamation of the gospel. It's something the disciples who were planning on going to Emmaus discovered all too well. Somewhere in the night, on the edge of Emmaus, they encountered the crucified-yet-risen Christ in such a powerful way that they were compelled to proclaim his resurrection as they made their way back to Jerusalem—in the dark.

Conclusion

So here we are: a people trudging along in silence. Sure, we've heard the Easter news, but it has failed to lift us, disappointed as we've been by the dashing of our hopes and dreams. But take heart! Christ joins us in that dour walk. Though he will not show us how to escape such walks, he will meet us and be with us there. And, frankly, that may be something worth talking about—regardless of the dark corner of the world you're in—even in the middle of the night.

CHAPTER FOUR

Pentecost:
A Jewish Spring
of the Church
Acts 2:1-21; 2:14-41; 2:42-47

Lectionary: Years A, B, and C, Pentecost
Year A, Second Sunday of Easter
Year A, Third Sunday of Easter
Year A, Fourth Sunday of Easter

INTRODUCTION

Acts 2 includes four lectionary readings from three distinct sections of the text (2:1-21; 14-41; 42-47) that, despite some overlap, have different yet not conflicting focuses. Therefore, I will attempt to analyze the chapter as a whole without neglecting its parts.

TEXT

[1]And when the day of Pentecost had come, they were all together in one place. [2]And suddenly a sound came from heaven like the rush of a mighty wind, and it filled all the house where they were sitting. [3]And there appeared to them tongues as of fire, distributed and resting on each one of them. [4]And they were all filled with the Holy Spirit and began to speak in tongues, as the Spirit gave them utterance.

[5]Now there were dwelling in Jerusalem Jews, devout men from every nation under heaven. [6]And at this sound the multitude came

together, and they were bewildered, because each one heard them speaking in his own language. [7]And they were amazed and wondered, saying, "Are not all these who are speaking Galileans? [8]And how is it that we hear, each one of us, in his own native language? [9]Parthians and Medes and Elamites and residents of Mesopotamia, Judea and Cappadocia, Pontus and Asia, [10]Phrygia and Pamphylia, Egypt and the parts of Libya belonging to Cyrene, and visitors from Rome, both Jews and proselytes, [11]Cretans and Arabians, we hear them telling in our own tongues the mighty works of God." [12]And all were amazed and perplexed, saying to one another, "What does this mean?" [13]But others mocking said, "They are filled with new wine."

[14]But Peter, standing with the eleven, lifted up his voice and addressed them, "Jews and all who dwell in Jerusalem, let this be known to you, and give ear to my words. [15]For these men are not drunk, as you suppose, since it is only the third hour of the day; [16]but this is what was spoken by the prophet Joel: [17] 'And in the last days it shall be, God declares, that I will pour out my spirit upon all flesh, and your sons and your daughters shall prophesy, and your young men shall see visions, and your old men shall dream dreams; [18]yea, and on my menservants and my maidservants in those days I will pour out my spirit; and they shall prophesy. [19]And I will show wonders in the heaven above and signs on the earth beneath, blood, and fire, and vapor of smoke; [20]the sun shall be turned into darkness and the moon into blood, before the day of the Lord comes, the great and manifest day. [21]And it shall be that whoever calls on the name of the Lord shall be saved.'

[22]"Israelites, hear these words: Jesus of Nazareth, a man attested to you by God with mighty works and wonders and signs which God did through him in your midst, as you yourselves know— [23]this man, delivered up according to the definite plan and foreknowledge of God, you crucified and killed by the hands of lawless men, [24]but him God raised up, having loosed the pangs of death, because it was not possible for him to be held by it. [25]For David says concerning him, 'I saw the Lord always before me, for he is at my right hand that I may not be shaken; [26]therefore my heart was glad, and my tongue rejoiced; moreover my flesh will dwell in hope. [27]For you will not abandon my soul to Hades, nor

let your holy one see corruption. [28]You have made known to me ways of life; you will make me full of gladness with your presence.'

[29]"Brethren, I may say this to you confidently of the patriarch David: that he both died and was buried, and his tomb is with us to this day. [30]Being therefore a prophet, and knowing that God had sworn with an oath to him that he would set one of his descendants upon his throne, [31]he foresaw and spoke of the resurrection of the Christ, that he was not abandoned to Hades, nor did his flesh see corruption. [32]This Jesus God raised up, and of that we all are witnesses. [33]Being therefore exalted at the right hand of God, and having received from the Father the promise of the Holy Spirit, he has poured out this which you see and hear. [34]For David did not ascend into the heavens; but he himself says, 'The Lord said to my Lord, Sit at my right hand, [35]till I make your enemies a stool for your feet.' [36]Let all the house of Israel therefore know assuredly that God has made him both Lord and Christ, this Jesus whom you crucified."

[37]Now when they heard this they were cut to the heart, and said to Peter and the rest of the apostles, "Brethren, what shall we do?" [38]And Peter said to them, "Repent, and be baptized every one of you in the name of Jesus Christ for the forgiveness of your sins; and you shall receive the gift of the Holy Spirit. [39]For the promise is to you and to your children and to all who are far off; everyone whom the Lord our God calls to him." [40]And he testified with many other words and exhorted them, saying, "Save yourselves from this crooked generation." [41]So those who received his word were baptized, and there were added that day about three thousand souls.

[42]And they devoted themselves to the apostles' teaching and fellowship, to the breaking of bread and the prayers. [43]And fear came upon every soul; and many wonders and signs were done through the apostles. [44]And all who believed were together and had all things in common; [45]and they sold their possessions and goods and distributed them to all, as any had need. [46]And day by day, attending the temple together and breaking bread in their homes, they partook of food with glad and generous hearts, [47]praising God and having favor with all the people. And the Lord added to their number day by day those who were being saved.

(Author's translation)

TWO PENTECOSTS—ONE FOR THE JEWS (ACTS 2) AND ONE FOR THE GENTILES (ACTS 10)

What would the feast of the Christian Pentecost be without the reading of Acts 2? It would be like celebrating Christmas without the birth narrative of Luke 2:1-20. Something really important would be missing: the foundational story. But if we read the Pentecost account in Acts carefully, then we will come to realize that only indirectly and subtly is it directed toward us Gentile Christians. Don't get me wrong: we Christians from the Gentile community have already been addressed, and thus will be included in God's covenant through Israel's hope, the Son of God and the Messiah, Jesus of Nazareth. This has been clear ever since Simeon praised God for sending Jesus to be Israel's universal consolation and salvation (Luke 2:22-35). But in spite of our shared perspective of Acts 2, this Pentecost story is not *really* ours, for it's more of a Jewish Pentecost. Our Pentecost comes when Cornelius and his house receive the Holy Spirit (Acts 10:44-48).

In other words, Luke tells two Pentecost stories, one for the Jews and one for the Gentiles. This may sound strange and a bit puzzling, but Luke has a reason for this kind of "sequel-ing." It has to do with his narratological concept—his mode of telling the story and his way of developing the plot. The first few chapters of the book of Acts narrate the great success of the gospel proclamation in Jerusalem. Literally thousands of Jews (Acts 2:41; 4:4; 5:14) are baptized and join the Christian community. It's basically a success story for the Christian gospel, in spite of the conflicts that the community will face. These conflicts come from outside (the Sadducees' denial of the hope of resurrection [Acts 4:1-2; cf. Acts 23:8] and because of jealousy [Acts 5:17] imprisoning the apostles [Acts 4:3; 5:18]) as well as from *inside* the early Christians' own "ideal" community (Ananias and Sapphira [Acts 5:1-11], Grecian-Jewish widows being neglected in the daily distribution of food [Acts 6:1-6]). In sum, despite the uproar and difficulties the early Christian community in Jerusalem faces, it's still a success story that we might call "the Jewish Spring of the Church."

This positive and bright side of the early Christianity narrated by Luke turns darker with the stoning of Stephen (Acts 7:54-60). The tone of the narrative sharpens. Stephen's harsh verbal attack on his Jewish audience in Acts 7:51-53 leads to his stoning (verses

54-60) and, as a consequence, all Christians being persecuted and expelled from Jerusalem except for the apostles (Acts 8:1). Their presence in Jerusalem is still needed. They represent an almost Vatican-like authority that will last until the apostolic council meeting (Acts 15). Peter in particular is the key apostolic figure. When Philip starts the Christian mission in Samaria, he is allowed to baptize; yet the Holy Spirit is bound to Peter. He has to come from Jerusalem to authorize the baptisms by laying his hands on the baptized, which action causes the Holy Spirit to be poured out (Acts 8:14-17). This has nothing to do with magic; instead, it demonstrates the divine authority the twelve are to exert. But the expulsion of Greek-speaking Jewish Christians (Hellenists) from Jerusalem also slowly leads Peter to cross geographic and ethnic boundaries. He becomes the first "official" to cross the boundary between Jews and Gentiles, which is marked by the dietary and cleansing rules of Torah, when he meets Cornelius and his Gentile household in Acts 10. The baptism of the Ethiopian eunuch in Acts 8:26-40 is but a preliminary step in the sending of the Christian gospel to the non-Jewish world. Cornelius becomes the first named Gentile Christian. God's Holy Spirit compels Peter to baptize Cornelius (Acts 10:44-48). Thus, it is appropriate to call this event the second Pentecost, the Pentecost for the Gentiles.

What does this mean for the interpretation of Acts 2? Do we still have the right to preach this text at Pentecost? Sure we do, and we should, because we Gentile Christians are intentionally addressed. Without this Jewish Pentecost, there would be no Gentile Christian Pentecost. Israel is the source and prime addressee of the gospel. This has already been made clear by Luke throughout the first half of his two-volume narrative. In order to remain crystal clear about this "two-step salvation program" (first Israel, then the Gentiles; cf. Paul's scheme to proclaim the gospel in Acts), he divides the coming of the Holy Spirit into two separate yet interrelated events.

How to Preach About Israel Nowadays?

What does all this mean for our preaching about Israel today? The situation has changed entirely since the time of the NT writers. The church has become an almost exclusively Gentile Christian church. Israel has continued its path to salvation by means of Torah, and it does not intend to take a different direction. Why should they? This may come as a surprise with regard to the NT writings. Don't they identify Israel as the prime addressee of the gospel? Yes, they do. In this respect, there is no basic difference between the Gospel writers and Paul, even in the much-debated chapters of Romans 9–11.[1] They all agree on this key issue: that the gospel is for all people, but that Israel is its prime addressee.

The issue raised in the NT, though, is why Israel has, for the most part, rejected this gospel. We could thus describe the NT writings as a grief document. The NT scriptures are an attempt to understand why the tragic split occurred between synagogue and church. The NT authors are tempted to place the blame on the Jewish side. Luke is no exception to this rule. He blames the Jewish leaders—or even the Jews in general—of jealousy, which causes them to speak against the gospel (Acts 5:17; 13:45). It's their false accusations (Acts 6:11-14) that lead to the dramatic stoning of Stephen. That Stephen's face looks "like the face of an angel" (verse 15) is but to underline his innocence. We as readers also know that the Lukan Paul is blameless. He is arrested while practicing a Jewish rite in the temple (Acts 21:27-36). The accusations against him are also false. Luke portrays Paul as a firm, believing Jewish Christian from the Pharisaic tradition (Acts 22:3; 23:6). Luke's portrayal of Paul is a polemic against the Jewish refusal of the Christian gospel and forms part of his narratological strategy of describing the rise of Christianity in light of the split Jewish reactions to the gospel.

When we read these texts and preach about them, we have to keep Luke's polemic in mind. We are called not to forget the painful tribulations of the Jews, especially in this past century, with their culmination in the horrors of the *Shoah*, or Holocaust. When we encounter Judaism, we have to do so with an attitude of mutual respect. The basis of the relationship must not be to assume that the other lacks something fundamental, but that we both are partners in need of God's grace and commandments. Neither Judaism nor Christianity is a deficient religion; they are different ways of living according to God's will. In other words, let us confess the basic elements of our faiths, allowing for differences where they occur, yet let us also make fruitful use of those differences. They are not a hindrance but an asset to dialogue and prayer! In sum: leave the question of ultimate truth (a Greek philosophical notion that has had a tremendous and sometimes detrimental influence on Christianity) open to God. Our knowledge and comprehension is much smaller than God's grace and love.

FIRST PROMISE FULFILLED: THE COMING OF THE HOLY SPIRIT TO ISRAEL (ACTS 2:1-13)

The Pentecost scene has to be interpreted in light of its announcement by the risen Christ, first in Luke 24:49 and then in Acts 1:4-5, 8. Thus, the coming of the Spirit is a promise fulfilled. It is the beginning of the end of time, an eschatological event that serves to restore *Israel* anew under the guidance of the Spirit. This restoration of Israel is less a political-messianic event than a salvific experience. It will include the Gentile world, even though their hour is still to come. The second promise has yet to be fulfilled (Acts 10).

When in the ascension scene the eleven ask Jesus, "Lord, is this the time when you will restore the kingdom to Israel?" (Acts 1:6), he becomes somewhat evasive. Instead of giving a clear yes or no, he replies that "it is not for you to know the times or periods that the Father has set by his own authority" (v. 7). Is it simply illegitimate for them to know the exact date, or is this reply an indirect repudiation of a view that sees Israel's restoration in political-messianic terms? In trying to find an answer to this question, one has to include verse 8, which is also part of Jesus' answer. Grammatically, the negation in verse 7—"it is not" (Greek *ouch*)—has its continuation in the particle "but" (Greek *alla*) of verse 8. Verse 7 is the negation and verse 8 marks the positive side of Jesus' answer. Thus, the emphasis lies on verse 8. The reception of the Spirit will not be something *less than*, but *different from* what was expected and hoped for. Since this promised event will not deny the validity of Israel's kingdom but redefine it, Jesus gives no simple yes or no answer to their question. Again, the Lukan Jesus has

to make strenuous ongoing efforts to teach even his closest followers that his salvation is not restricted to a political-messianic act,
but that the restoration of Israel means the fulfillment of Israel's
long-awaited hope for resurrection; and this hope fulfilled also
reaches out to and includes the Gentile world.

The Greek phrase *en to symplerousthai ten hemeran tes pentekostes*,
with which Luke begins the Pentecost scene in Acts 2:1, literally
translates as "when the day of Pentecost was being fulfilled." It
underscores the fact that now the time of (first) fulfillment has
come. Pentecost, which means "fiftieth day," is named after the
first Jewish harvest feast of the year. It comes fifty days after
Passover, and since Jesus died and rose again during Passover, this
time span also reflects the fifty days since Easter. Thus,
Christianity has appropriated the name of a Jewish feast by calling
the day of the coming of the Holy Spirit Pentecost. Whether this is
a coincidence or was intentionally placed here by the author—or
even whether it is historically accurate—remains an open question. At any rate, it helps to explain the presence of the many Jews
"from every nation under heaven" (Acts 2:5). The international
flair of the scene fits nicely Luke's narratological strategy. It's also
worth noting that the coming of the Spirit does not occur in the
temple, which has been of key interest in the plot thus far. The
eleven stayed "continually in the temple blessing God" (Luke
24:53) after Jesus ascended into heaven, but now they have left this
holy Jewish place, and all are gathered in a house (Acts 2:2).
Whether this "all" (Greek *pantes* in v. 1) refers to the twelve apostles (cf. v. 14) or to the 120 brethren (Acts 1:15) is unknown. At any
rate, the twelve play an important role. They represent the twelve
tribes of Israel, and therefore the disgraced Judas had to be
replaced by someone who was a "witness" of the resurrection
(Acts 1:22).

Luke describes the sudden sounds (Acts 2:2) and sights (v. 3) as
manifestations of the Spirit. Being filled with the Holy Spirit
enables them "to speak in tongues" (v. 4), which here means the
sudden ability to speak different languages. What amazes the people at the scene is that they hear Galileans speaking their own
native languages (v. 8). This does not call so much for interpretation (cf. Paul in 1 Cor. 14:27) as it does for explanation: "What does

this mean?" (Acts 2:12). The people are in part "amazed and per-plexed." Others try to ridicule the apostles: "They are filled with new wine" (v. 13). Peter will soon have to stand up to explain—and what a sermon they will hear!

Before we can focus on Peter's speech, we need to move back to the list of the nations and the lands (Acts 2:9-11). Anybody who has been asked to read it at Pentecost knows it's a tongue twister. The list is there to demonstrate the universal side of Judaism. Jerusalem is home not only for Jews from Judea and Galilee, but also for many international Jews, the so-called Diaspora Jews. Some of them are even explicitly labeled as nonresidents (Greek *epidemountes*; v. 10)—as visitors or guests from Rome, for example. The list is designed to represent a kind of totality of the then-known *oikomene*, the inhabited, civilized world around the Mediterranean. What is important, though, is that only Jews are mentioned here. Verse 5 speaks of Jews who have always lived in Jerusalem and those who have either moved there from some-where else in the Diaspora or who are only there as visitors. Robert Tannehill is right when he states that "the presence of Jews from every nation under heaven at Pentecost introduces a . . . symbolic dimension into that narrative, suggesting first that it is the goal of the gospel to address all Israel, scattered throughout the world, and second that it must also address the gentile inhabitants of the lands from which these Jews come."[2] The distinction between "Jews and proselytes" in verse 10 is one of ethnic background but not of religious attitude, for male proselytes have become Jews by the act of circumcision. Thus, in sum, only Jews are present and are witnesses of this surprising spiritual event.

CLARIFICATION AND THE CALL FOR REPENTANCE: PETER'S PENTECOST SPEECH (ACTS 2:14-41)

The situation caused by the manifestation of the Spirit now calls for explanation. Thus Peter, standing amidst the other eleven, will speak on their behalf. Whereas the crowd gathered in the house is puzzled and amazed, the apostles seem to know exactly what has happened. The time of fulfillment has come. The interim period of waiting "in the city until you are clothed with power from on high" (Luke 24:49; cf. Acts 1:8) is finally over. The time when they themselves were so much in need of remedial teaching from Jesus (Luke 24) has vanished. In this respect, they have taken over the role and responsibility Jesus exercised while he was among them. Now Peter plays the key role. His speech is one of the longest in Acts. It seems as if he has been waiting a long time for this moment to occur. He is well prepared, and what a skilled homiletician and preacher he is!

Peter's speech moves backward chronologically. He starts by replying to the mockery (v. 15), then interprets the manifestation of the Spirit as a fulfillment of Joel's prophecy (vv. 16-21), and moves on to a rather comprehensive treatment of Jesus' death and resurrection (vv. 22-36). This, then, will be enough for the moment; the crowd will have to react, and their response determines the further outline and outcome of this first Christian mission attempt.

The accusation of drunkenness is an easy charge to counter. The reasoning that this is only "the third hour of the day" (v. 15), or nine o'clock in the morning, should suffice. What has been misunderstood as mere drunkenness is in fact a manifestation of the Spirit. As strange as these signs may appear to this Jewish crowd, they nonetheless perfectly fit the long-awaited Jewish hopes and dreams. Everything that is happening now was to be expected. What is transpiring is the beginning of "the last days" (v. 17), just as Joel long ago prophesied. The original Greek *en tais eschatais hemerais* for "the last days" leaves no doubt as to what time period has just begun: the *eschaton*. It's noteworthy that Luke here exchanges *en tais eschatais hemerais* for the original *meta tauta*, which merely means "after this" and thus is a much more vague and imprecise expression. Conzelmann, by the way, in his commentary on Acts, apparently feels uneasy about this change because, contrary to his own view, this is an indication that there is an eschatological side to Luke's theology—even if it does not stand in the foreground as much as it does in Paul's theology, which was formulated at least one generation before Luke.[3] Different times require different attitudes and solutions.

At any rate, what is crucial here and always will be for the narrator's argument is that everything that happens is in complete agreement with and fulfillment of biblical prophecies. There will be only one exception to this rule, at the end of Peter's mission speech to Cornelius in Acts 10, but this complex situation will be resolved when the circumstances demand a solution. Even then, the outcome will be a surprising one (see chapter 6).

The outpouring of the Spirit is the beginning of a new age, the last to come before the end of days. The present times of the Spirit are not yet identical with the last, eschatological "day of the Lord" (Acts 2:20) that will be introduced and accompanied by dramatic cosmological signs and wonders in heaven and on earth (vv. 19-20). These days represent the interim and include the introductory events that will lead up to the final "great and manifest" day of the Lord (v. 20), which will be a day of judgment. The first signs of this interim come as a relief, a time when dreams come true. This new age is described in rather poetic ways: "Your sons and your daughters shall prophesy, and your young men shall see visions, and your old men shall dream dreams" (vv. 17-18). The linguistic miracle occurring among them is interpreted prophetically. The Christian Pentecost unites people and brings them together—in stark contrast to the result of the building of the tower of Babel (Gen. 11). This is but the first step in God's much larger scheme of salvation for the world. The outpouring of the Spirit will spread to "all flesh" (Acts 2:17), thus having a worldwide effect and eventually reaching and including the Gentile world. The quotation from Joel, which starts in verse 17 on this universal note, ends in a similar way: "And it shall be that whoever calls on the name of the Lord shall be saved." This inclusion motif demonstrates how central the universal side of his theological program is for Luke. It also tells his readers that faith in Jesus does not involve merely joining a new Jewish group such as the Pharisees or Sadducees. It declares instead that whoever calls on Jesus' name admits a need for salvation. The Lukan Jesus has already proclaimed what this means, namely, "repentance and forgiveness of sins" (Luke 24:47). Peter will affirm the same thing in his sermons, as Luke's readers will discover (Acts 2:38).

Joel's prophecy is the scriptural background for the Jewish audience's understanding of the manifestation of the Spirit, but they need further information. This is the perfect opportunity for Peter to refer to Jesus, including his life, death, and resurrection, in order to prove literally to the Jews that by raising Jesus from the dead, "God has made him both Lord and Christ" (v. 36). This speech/sermon comes across not so much as an invitation than as a powerful proclamation of ultimate truth. It is less an appeal than a warning, an urgent call to redirect one's own life—in other words, a call to repentance. The scriptural evidence is overwhelming. It reads like a proof text for Christ's resurrection. Peter quotes from the Psalms, whose authorship traditionally was ascribed to King David at that time. This text (vv. 25-28 are from Ps. 16:8-11) is brought in as a key piece of christological evidence that Peter interprets as confirmation that David "foresaw and spoke of the resurrection of the Christ" (v. 31). When David says that his "flesh will dwell in hope" (v. 26), he refers not to his own resurrection but to that of the Christ who is also David's hope, the hope for resurrection. Since David "both died and was buried, and his tomb is with us to this day" (v. 29), he neither was raised nor did he ascend into heaven. But this is precisely the place to which Jesus has been exalted. That's why the disciples can receive from heaven the promise of the Spirit, which now has been poured out (v. 33) among them. Thus, it is conclusively proven that "God has made him both Lord and Christ, this Jesus whom you crucified" (v. 36).

This speech may be intended to be a missionary sermon, but its tone is striking. There is no attempt on Peter's part to win the audience by charming them and fishing for compliments as, for example, the Lukan Paul does when he defends himself before King Agrippa and Festus (Acts 26:2-3). No, Peter is harsh in tone and temper. There is no reason for him to be less than frank. The Jewish audience comes under heavy attack because they reacted to Jesus—in spite of all the "mighty works and wonders and signs" God did in their midst through him, "as you yourselves know" (v. 22)—with denial and rejection. Moreover, they actively took part in the accusations in his trial before Pilate (Luke 23:13-25), and thus are to be held responsible for Jesus' death. Twice, in the beginning and at the very end, Peter indicts them directly: "*You* crucified and killed" Jesus (Acts 2:23, 36; emphasis added).[4]

Although there is no excuse for Jewish complicity in the crucifixion, it will not be fatal for them because first, they will get the chance to repent (v. 38), and second, Jesus' death was no accident, but part of God's saving plan. Ironically, by doing evil they actually participated in a good cause. As Joseph said to his brothers, "Even though you intended to do harm to me, God intended it for good" (Gen. 50:20). Further, Peter can sound much more understanding at times, such as when he excuses his Jewish brethren: "I know that you acted in ignorance, as did also your rulers" (Acts 3:17). The narrator never makes any negative ontological statements about "the Jews" (as, for example, the Gospel of John does). Wherever Luke sounds polemical, as in Acts 2:23 and 36 (and especially in Acts 3:23; 7:51-59; 21:27-36; and 28:25-28), the Jewish people are not forever excluded from salvation. They still get a second and even a third chance. Thus, at the very end of the narrative, in spite of their ongoing attitude of rejection, the door to salvation in Christ still remains open for Jews, as well. Paul welcomes "all" (Greek *pantes*)—Gentiles and Jews (in this order from now on!)—who come and want to see him (28:30).

Apparently, the Jewish audience is willing to accept such strong statements because they are "cut to the heart" (v. 37). This is their first sign of repentance. They ask, "Brethren, what shall we do?" (v. 37). These words sound familiar. They are identical to the crowd's reply to John the Baptist's harsh words about them in Luke 3:7. Being called a "brood of vipers" does not come across as a compliment at all, does it? There are a couple of similarities between the two speeches. Both speakers attack their Jewish audience: John warns them not to trust in their natural descent as children of Abraham (v. 8), whereas Peter holds his audience responsible for Jesus' death. But instead of being put off, both crowds show a willingness to repent: "What [then] shall we do?" (Luke 3:10, 12, 14; Acts 2:37). Thus, there follows the call to repentance, which is a call to baptism. But where John the Baptist calls for a baptism of water (a baptism of repentance to prepare the way for the one who is mightier [Luke 3:16]), the baptism Peter calls for is that which comes as the fulfillment of the Baptist's prophecy—that is, a baptism of "the Holy Spirit and fire" (Luke 3:16). Baptism in the name of Jesus, leading to the repentance of sins, comes with the gift of God's Spirit (Acts 2:38). A change of attitude and mind is needed: "Save yourselves from this crooked generation" (v. 40).

The call to Christ is a call to salvation, a call to change one's own heart and mind. Again there is a hint of the universal side of the gospel. The promise of the Spirit is not given to Israel alone but also to "all who are far off" (Greek: *pasin tois eis makran*; v. 39). This remark does not cause any question or opposition here; it is an accepted announcement. Later on, when Paul has to defend his Gentile mission in almost identical terms (he was sent by the risen Lord to the "Gentiles far away" [Greek: *eis ethne makran*; 22:21]), the crowd yells, "Away with such a fellow from the earth! For he should not be allowed to live" (v. 22). Peter's sermon, however, is a tremendous success. There is no opposition whatsoever! No Jewish leaders who incite conflict, no envy, no jealousy. This will change soon, but for now let's rejoice and celebrate and welcome the new members of the Christian congregation, for "about three thousand souls" (Acts 2:41) are baptized that Pentecost in Jerusalem. What a great success! Multitudes of people join the Christian community. Luke loves big numbers, and he pushes all the narrative buttons in order to underline this success story. The Jewish spring of the church has arrived—no question about that! Everybody in Jerusalem seems to live in perfect—that is, in Christian—harmony. Paradise is so close you can taste it.

A DREAM COME TRUE: THE FIRST CHRISTIAN COMMUNITY IN JERUSALEM (ACTS 2:42-47)

Here, described in a nutshell, is an ideal Christian community. But is it too perfect to be believed? There is a similar kind of summary in Acts 4:32-35. The healing story and gospel proclamation in the temple in Acts 3 will generate the first strong opposition from the Sadducees and will lead to the first imprisonment (4:1-3); further, the second summary is followed by the first conflict story from within the Christian community (5:1-12). This is not accidental. It demonstrates that the early Christian church had to face conflict and tension. As much as those two summaries emphasize the ideal of communal spirit, they also are very aware of the realities of life with which the early church had to cope. Whether this ideal had any historical basis may be doubtful, but to put it aside on this ground is not justified. Luke exhorts his readers not to cling foolishly to an ideal that may never be fully realized, but to be summoned by it. His exhortations are directed more toward people with some wealth than toward the poor (who could not as easily afford to share what they had), but they are clear and serve to disturb us. Whoever stops dreaming (cf. 2:17) and striving to make dreams come true stops counting on the power of God's Spirit.

HOMILETIC POSSIBILITIES FOR PENTECOST: A JEWISH SPRING OF THE CHURCH

Günter's exegesis invites us to rethink our relationship to this foundational Pentecost text. What we might do is begin with how people hear this text (as the church's birthday), and move toward refiguring it as a Jewish-Christian birthday party to which we have been invited, not so much as the guests of honor, but as fellow celebrants. In this way, we can reenvision Pentecost as a shared reality rather than merely as an in-house Gentile Christian observance.

Introduction

Here we should start by painting the picture from the text and comparing it to an unusual birthday party. It might look something like this:

> Imagine a family with an unusual way of observing birthdays. Whenever one of their number celebrates another year of life, they invite friends and family to be seated at a big round table. At every place around the table are balloons, colorful plates, even a little gift. So no matter who you are, this birthday party would have something for you, too. Of course, there's confusion in the mayhem of the moment. More than once, guests new to this birthday custom would be heard asking the question, "Just whose birthday is this, anyway?" Well, if you can imagine that, perhaps you can envision what the first Pentecost was like. We call Pentecost "the church's

birthday." Yet the celebration scene looks unlike most parties we know. There are no cake candles for the birthday boy, but there are tongues of fire for each guest. And as for the gift, there's only one given: the Holy Spirit, which is for everyone, too. Maybe on Pentecost, we too should ask, "Just whose birthday is this, anyway?"

Scene 1
On closer inspection, we must admit that this Pentecost birthday is decidedly Jewish.

Here we simply lay out the text with a little explanation. One might begin by talking about Pentecost as a Jewish holiday, a harvest feast connected to a celebration of the giving of the Law. Here preachers should be careful not to talk about the Law as a burden or as a kind of legalistic foil to the gospel. Instead, one might even talk about the Jewish celebration *"Simhat Torah,"* or "Rejoice in the Law," in which people actually dance with the Torah scroll in celebration. From there preachers could then talk about the picture drawn in Luke-Acts. Remember, the gathered disciples are still all Jews. Moreover, the international pilgrims who witness the events, ask the questions, and hear the gospel preached in their own tongues are all Jews or Jewish proselytes. From beginning to end, this Pentecost scene is Jewish: Jews are portrayed as celebrating, questioning, and receiving God's good gifts. We have a birthday party here, all right, but a decidedly *Jewish* one.

Scene 2
Guess that makes us guests at the Spirit's party.

Of course, the fact that the party is Jewish does not mean we are utterly left out. We know in our study of Luke-Acts that this is the first of a two-part Spirit gift (see chapter 6). Moreover, as readers of the story, we have the joy of overhearing and glimpsing God's Spirit at work. The key for us Gentile Christians is not to assume we're in charge or the center of attention. It might be good for us, even this day, to remind ourselves of the grace of God by which we were adopted into this joyful family.

"Guest"? Just a guest? Of course, part of us rebels at the idea. We've become so accustomed to the notion that Pentecost is *our* day, we never stopped to look closely at the other people in attendance. Yet it's not all so bad. Perhaps by realizing who is actually there, we can revel in the moment. After all, it's not a bad thing to be a guest at someone else's party—especially when God is the one throwing it!

How did Bible scholar Krister Stendahl put it? We are, at best, "honorary Jews."[5] It is enough to enjoy the participation we have, to say please and thank you as the moment warrants, and above all, to share in the joy of being part of God's celebration, even if we're not the center of attention. Perhaps there is a special joy in being graciously seated around a table big enough for everyone. Maybe there is a greater freedom than fencing off the happiness of me and mine from that of others: the joyful sharing of us and ours in the presence of a God who gives the Spirit in ever-novel ways.

Scene 3
Such a bizarre party prompts questions:
What does this mean?

By now we should be rightly confused. This shared joy in the Spirit is not the way of the world we know. Here preachers should explore the opposite of the Pentecost scene. Our lives usually proceed by a careful cost-benefit analysis. For us, joy is not joy unless it is possessed. It is either the deserved fruit of our labors or it is private property, properly fenced off with the requisite deeds and titles to show ownership. To ask "What does this mean?" is to ask a profoundly honest question. The gathered crowd had it right on a purely human level. When they saw the Spirit manifested on Pentecost, they thought it could only be an aberration: early morning drunkenness from partygoers who didn't know when to lay off the wine. To pose the question is to be troubled by that which cannot be calculated or managed. Looking at this Pentecost party, it's only natural to wonder, "What does this mean?"

Scene 4
Peter gives the answer: God is creating all things anew.

The answer is important here. It represents, theologically, a profound sense of divine time. We monitor time in equal units of identical duration, but this is not God's way. Now is "high time," new creation time—the time of eschatological fulfillment.

Peter's is an odd speech, but it is important not to miss it. Please note how he helps to explain. What happened here is no accident, no partying without a license. Indeed, what happens on Pentecost is part of God's plan to remake creation. At the very point that we think it's time to turn down the volume, send the revelers home, and cut off the free food and wine, God is just getting started. How do we know? The heavens are changing. And the earth . . . well, *the earth is next!* You see, this odd sharing of the Spirit at a kind of birthday bash is not an end, but a new beginning that can't be controlled by the people who make you punch time clocks or by the bean counters. They're too busy looking backward at who gets what. God's party in the Spirit points ahead to something new: a new order in which there's enough for everybody, a new age in which the party is not the exception, but the rule!

Scene 5
Of course, this means that we have to break with our deadly ways.

Here it's important to remember that Peter's sermon is also a call to repentance. Although Peter's answer essentially blames the Jews for Christ's death, we preachers of the gospel do not have to take the same route. To talk about the need for repentance and turning from our deadly ways is just another way of saying that the forces in our world that wish to destroy God's plan are still with us. Although for us, Jesus' death on the cross is the central manifestation of the reality that God is making all things new, evil still manages to find ways of trying to grind up the strange freedom and joy of God—often by working through us and our vested interests. The key here for the preacher is to help us see those places where God's new creation evokes an awareness in us (as opposed to someone else) that we are to repent. In this way, moreover, repentance is not a prerequisite, but an after-effect of divine grace. God is in the new creation mode, so why should we persist in propping up the death-dealing ways of the old order?

Conclusion
Imagine that: a birthday party in which you don't have to blow out the candles!

With this conclusion we return to the party image. Above all, the focus must continue on divine grace, because apart from this, we simply return to our typically Protestant works-righteousness assembly line.

So, imagine that: a birthday party in which you don't have to blow out the candles! The Spirit wants to keep the party going permanently. Sure, it's not easy to think of giving up the perks that come with business as usual: the Israelites called them Egyptian fleshpots, we call them pensions and productivity bonuses. God's party in the Spirit invites us, however, to envision something new: a world in which God's people, the Jews, can live without fear, and a world in which we Gentile Christians don't need to be in control, but can live in the Spirit's joy for one another in the community of our dreams.

CHAPTER FIVE

The Persecuted Persecutor: The Conversion of Paul

Acts 9:1-31

Lectionary: Year C, Third Sunday of Easter

TEXT

¹But Saul, still breathing threats and murder against the disciples of the Lord, went to the high priest ²and asked him for letters to the synagogues at Damascus, so that in case he found any belonging to the Way, men or women, he might bring them bound to Jerusalem. ³Now as he journeyed he approached Damascus, and suddenly a light from heaven flashed around him; ⁴and falling to the ground, he heard a voice saying to him, "Saul, Saul, why do you persecute me?" ⁵He said, "Who are you, Lord?" He said, "I am Jesus, whom you persecute, ⁶but rise and enter the city, and you will be told what you are to do." ⁷The men who were traveling with him stood speechless, hearing the voice but seeing no one. ⁸Saul arose from the ground, and when his eyes were opened, he could see nothing. Leading him by the hand, they brought him into Damascus. ⁹And for three days he was without sight, and neither ate nor drank.

¹⁰Now there was a disciple in Damascus named Ananias, and the Lord said to him in a vision, "Ananias!" And he said, "Here I

am, Lord." [11]And the Lord said to him, "Rise and go to the street called the Straight, and inquire in the house of Judas for a man from Tarsus named Saul; for behold, he is praying, [12]and he has seen a man named Ananias come in and lay his hands on him so that he might regain his sight." [13]But Ananias answered, "Lord, I have heard from many about this man, how much evil he has done to your saints in Jerusalem. [14]And here he has authority from the chief priests to bind all who call upon your name." [15]But the Lord said to him, "Go, for he is a chosen instrument of mine to carry my name before the Gentiles and the kings and the sons [children] of Israel; [16]for I myself will show him how much he must suffer for the sake of my name." [17]So Ananias departed and entered the house. And laying his hands on him he said, "Brother Saul, the Lord has sent me, Jesus who appeared to you on the way by which you came, so that you regain your sight and be filled with the Holy Spirit." [18]And immediately something like scales fell from his eyes, he regained sight, got up and was baptized, [19]and took food and was strengthened. For several days he was with the disciples in Damascus, [20]and immediately he proclaimed Jesus in the synagogues, saying, "He is the Son of God." [21]And all who heard him were perplexed, and said, "Is not this the man who destroyed those in Jerusalem who called upon this name, and has come here for this purpose to bring them bound to the chief priests?" [22]But Saul increased all the more in strength, and confounded the Jews who lived in Damascus by proving that Jesus is the Christ.

[23]When many days had passed the Jews plotted to kill him, [24]but their plot became known to Saul. They were watching the gates day and night, to kill him. [25]And his disciples took him by night and let him down over the wall, lowering him in a basket.

[26]And when he had come to Jerusalem he attempted to join the disciples; and all were afraid of him, not believing that he was a disciple. [27]But Barnabas took him, and brought him to the apostles, and declared to them how on the road he had seen the Lord and that he spoke to him and how at Damascus he had proclaimed boldly in the name of Jesus. [28]So he went in and out with them at Jerusalem, proclaiming boldly in the name of the Lord. [29]And he spoke and disputed against the Hellenists; but they were seeking to kill him. [30]When the brethren learned about it, they brought him

down to Caesarea, and sent him off to Tarsus. ³¹Thus, the church throughout Judea and Galilee and Samaria had peace; it was built up and walked in the fear of the Lord. And with the comfort of the Holy Spirit it was multiplied. (Author's translation)

INTRODUCTION

Acts 9 consists of two lessons in the lectionary. From a narrative point of view, however, one should not divide the chapter and separate it into different stories. Verses 20-26 are to be included, for they form a necessary link in the course of the plot, and build up to the summary in 9:31. The ironic meaning of the "peace" of the Christian community in 9:31 is only fully understood if verses 20-26 are not left out. That chapter 9 should be read as one piece becomes even more obvious when one attempts to determine the end of the conversion story. Where does it actually end, after verse 19*a*, 19*b*, or 20? But what about the following verses, 21 and 22? Doesn't it make sense to hear from the narrator how the Christian Jews react to the converted Saul? If Ananias finds it difficult to welcome Saul at first, then what about the rest of the Jewish Christian community at Damascus? Thus, 9:22 would make a more appropriate ending for the conversion narrative.

The fact that Luke retells Paul's conversion twice in his narrative, in Acts 22 and 26, should not be overlooked. To view the three conversion narratives in Acts under the premise of different sources or traditions, however, will lead to a dead end. Luke has not incorporated three different accounts of the same event into his narrative. Rather, one has to question the literary function of the three narratives. Thus viewed, each of these accounts discloses a distinct meaning. The first unit in Acts 9 reports the event itself, as it "really" happened, using traditional legendary material that must have been circulating, as Paul himself indicates in his own report about his conversion/call in Galatians 1:13: "You have heard, no doubt, of my earlier life in Judaism. I was violently persecuting the church of God and was trying to destroy it." The exact amount of this traditional legendary material in Acts is difficult to determine. The figure of Ananias could be historical, but the wording of the dialogues that he has with the Exalted One and with Paul most likely is not. Verses 15-16 in particular seem to be from Luke himself because they are so very programmatic for the overall portrait of his narrative figure, Paul.

The account in Acts 22 is told from a different narratorial perspective. Whereas in Acts 9 the narrator tells the story in the distant third person singular—that is, in an "objective" manner—in Acts 22, we learn how Paul himself experienced his conversion with all its consequences. The setting of the account is also important: Paul has just been falsely arrested by a Jewish mob (21:27-36). He's in a critical, life-threatening situation as he begins his speech, which literally takes on the form of a "defense" (22:1). Paul is innocent. He has not betrayed Judaism. His Jewish brethren should know better, for it was he who witnessed and approved of the stoning of Stephen (v. 20; cf. 8:1). But it was the Lord himself who told him, "Go, for I will send you far away to the Gentiles" (22:21; Greek: *eis ethne makran*; cf. chapter 4). This last remark about the Gentiles causes tremendous uproar and anger, and the Jews want to assassinate him (vv. 22-24; cf. 23:12-22).

The picture has changed somewhat in Acts 26. Paul defends himself before King Agrippa and the Roman procurator Festus, but his speech before the two highest political authorities in the region turns into an outright confession of the Christian faith, which is fundamentally Jewish; thus, their reaction speaks for itself. Whereas Festus declares Paul to be mad (26:24), Agrippa finds Paul persuasive: "Are you so quickly persuading me to become a Christian?" (v. 28). Paul is innocent of apostasy and political rioting, and he should be set free. But since he had appealed to the emperor, he has to be sent to Rome to defend his case there (v. 32; cf. 25:11-12). In moving from true legend (Acts 9) to defense speech (Acts 22) to confession and proclamation of the Christian gospel (Acts 26), Luke engages in a kind of "sequel-ing" that is intentional. It prepares the reader for the end of the narrative where Paul, having arrived in Rome and in spite of his arrest, is portrayed as a bold and unhindered messenger of and for the gospel (Acts 28:30). This boldness is the legacy that the Lukan readers ought to live up to.

THE DISTINCTION BETWEEN THE PAUL OF THE LETTERS AND THE LUKAN PAUL: AN IMPORTANT DIFFERENCE IN HERMENEUTICAL PERSPECTIVE

Before we look at the narrative interpretation of Paul's conversion in Acts 9, one important hermeneutical statement has to be made. There is a fundamental difference between the Paul of the letters and the Paul according to Acts. Christian tradition has tended to mix the two and thereby create a kind of harmonized Paul who is neither Pauline nor Lukan. It is difficult to separate the two Pauls, but it is important to keep them apart in order to do justice to each. If we proceed as historians, we will have to focus on Paul's own writings—there is no question about this. Although Paul did not write an autobiography, his undisputed letters (1 Thessalonians, 1 and 2 Corinthians, Philemon, Galatians, Philippians, and Romans) contain important biographical material that can shed light on Paul's life and background and allow us to reconstruct much of his missionary travels.[1] Some of his material stands in open conflict with Luke's portrayal of him. To give but a small example, Paul mentions only three visits to Jerusalem: one about three years after his conversion/call (Gal. 1:18), then one about fourteen years later on behalf of the so-called apostolic council meeting (Gal. 2:1), and one last visit, which he announces in his Letter to the Romans (15:25). The notes in Galatians 1 and 2 are of special value. Paul's own record is to be trusted because he must be correct on the dates for the sake of his argument against the so-called Judaizers. For Paul to suppress mention of a visit that actually had taken place would be fatal to his line of argument, which asserts that he has remained independent from the Jerusalem church authorities. He regards himself as equal to Peter and James (Gal. 2:7-10).

Luke, though, knows of at least five visits to Jerusalem by Paul: the first after his conversion (Acts 9:26), a second with Barnabas to deliver a special collection for the sake of famine relief (Acts 11:30), a third on behalf of the apostolic council meeting (Acts 15), a fourth to fulfill a Jewish repentance rite (Acts 18:22-23), and a fifth during which he is arrested in the temple (Acts 21:15-36). If we give at least literary credence to the report in Acts that he "was brought up in this city at the feet of Gamaliel" (22:3), this then would be his sixth—and by far longest—stay in Jerusalem and makes this city Paul's second hometown. Combined with the introduction of Saul as a witness to the stoning of Stephen in Acts 8:1, this reference could also make this sixth stay his first, assuming that he was still under the spiritual guidance and education of his teacher, Gamaliel. It is obvious that this difference in story line between Luke on the one hand and Paul himself on the other cannot be harmonized and has to be explained (see the Exegetical Introduction).

Another example of the differences between Luke and Paul can be seen in the narration of the conversion. Although the Paul of the letters refers to his call indirectly quite often, he actually mentions the specific event only once, and this only in two small verses in Galatians 1:15-16: "But when God, who had set me apart before I was born and called me through his grace, was pleased to reveal his Son to me, so that I might proclaim him among the Gentiles. . . ." Where or when exactly this happened we are not told, but from verse 17 we can infer that it happened near Damascus. Beyond that, we learn that Paul had been a zealous Jew persecuting the church (v. 13). That's it. What's even more important is that Paul describes Christ's revelation to him near Damascus in prophetic terms as a call resembling Jeremiah's. Thus, it is highly debatable whether one should even label it a conversion, which it clearly is in Acts 9, even though Paul himself can describe his former life in Judaism in pretty negative terms (Phil. 3:7-8). To sum up, in spite of the fact that both authors speak about the same person, the two different Pauls ought to be kept apart and separated!

SAUL AND PAUL: A LUKAN PLAY ON WORDS

We are used to speaking about the two different names for Paul, one before his conversion, "Saul," and one after, "Paul," the Greek translation of his Hebrew name. It is Luke who is responsible for this difference in names, a difference that has become a popular saying, "from Saul to Paul," which means a complete turnaround of someone's attitude or opinion. This fits nicely into the Lukan portrait of Paul. But this name change is a pure literary fiction and has no background in reality whatsoever. The Diaspora Jew Paul from Tarsus (Acts 9:11; 22:3) was brought up in a bicultural environment. Consequently, he spoke both Greek and Hebrew but had only one name, Saul. In Greek, the name Saul becomes Paul. Luke uses this play on words as a literary tool to illustrate the two different, almost opposite sides of Paul: his Jewish background and his Christian identity.

ON THE ROAD TO DAMASCUS: THE PERSECUTOR REDUCED TO NOTHINGNESS (ACTS 9:1-20)

Saul, on his way to Damascus, is already a known figure to the Lukan readers. Luke introduces him as a witness of the stoning of Stephen, and even though he remains passive there, the narrator nonetheless emphasizes that Saul "approved of" Stephen's death (Acts 8:1). Again, regardless of whether this anecdote is historical or not, what is important from a narrative point of view is that it's told. This episode makes perfect sense when compared to the overall portrait of the Lukan Paul. Luke takes pains to root Paul as deeply within Judaism as possible. Portraying Paul as a zealous Jew who persecutes the church before he is converted to faith in Christ makes more sense to readers who are skeptical of Paul and accuse him of apostasy and heresy. Paul mentions that he was a persecutor in his own writings (Gal. 1:13, Phil. 3:6). It's a known fact and part of the legend on which Luke then elaborates. The scene showing Paul witnessing and consenting to the death of Stephen is an ideal introduction to this narrative figure. It puts him on the side of the Jewish opponents of the Christian faith. If such a vigorous antagonist can be converted from persecutor to proclaimer of the gospel, he becomes a role model for someone who is skeptical about Paul's theology, who asks whether his theology remains truthful to Judaism or not (see the Exegetical Introduction)—and of course it does, there is no question about it!

The narrated Saul must have been actively involved in the persecutions of the church that arose in the aftermath of Stephen's martyrdom (Acts 8:1), because Luke introduces him in chapter 9 as "still breathing threats and murder against the disciples of the Lord" (v. 1). This man's emotions must have been volatile, for he is full of hate for "the Way," the Christian faith and proclamation. Saul is presented not only as a man of words, but as a man of deeds and action, as well. Thus, he goes to the high priest and asks him for letters to the synagogues at Damascus, which would allow him to persecute Christ's followers even there, arrest them, and bring them back to Jerusalem. Historically, such letters from the high priest don't seem plausible because the Jerusalem temple authorities had no jurisdictional power over the synagogues at Damascus. Judaism does not have a centralized institution as does, for example, the Roman Catholic Church with the Vatican. Each of the synagogue communities tended to mind its own business. Thus, no interference from Jerusalem would be allowed. But from a narrative point of view, this effort on Saul's part underlines his trustworthiness. He wants to be reckoned as an utterly loyal, faithful, and zealous Jew. This, by the way, remains Paul's view up to the very end, when in Rome he declares that in proclaiming Jesus as the Christ he has done "nothing against our [Jewish] people or the customs of our ancestors" (Acts 28:17). If there is a consistency in Luke's portrait of Paul, it is that Paul always sees himself as being a good Pharisaic Jew, first by persecuting the church, then by proclaiming Christ.

Saul receives permission to carry out what he thinks should be his duty as a faithful Jew and sets out on this grim journey to Damascus, when all of a sudden a flashing light from heaven strikes him and makes him fall to the ground. He hears a voice saying, "Saul, Saul, why do you persecute me?" Saul replies, "Who are you, Lord?" The voice reveals itself: "I am Jesus, whom you persecute." This self-revelation, which soon will be followed by a second one to Ananias with regard to Paul's call (vv. 15-16), is the only one in all of Acts in which the exalted Christ specifically identifies himself, thus putting Paul in a very special position! It becomes even more revealing in light of Luke 24:47, in which the risen Christ announces the coming inclusion of the Gentiles into God's covenant with Israel. It is Paul who is going to be the one to carry out this final, unfulfilled missionary goal! This makes him unique even with respect to the Lukan Peter. Peter's importance and authority are unquestioned, yet it's Paul who is given this special revelation by the risen Lord himself. The idea that Luke is aiming at subordinating the Gentile mission of Paul in favor of Peter's mission to Israel is wrong.[2] Although it is true that Luke seems reluctant to apply the title "apostle" to Paul and reserves it for the twelve who were with Jesus from the beginning (cf. Acts 1:21-22), one should not overlook the fact that even Luke refers twice to Paul as an apostle (in connection with Barnabas, Acts 14:4,14). From Paul's own writings we learn that he always stresses the point of his apostleship (for example, 1 Cor. 9:1-2; 15:9). Further, if Paul's apostleship was under dispute in Luke's time and Luke is setting out to defend Paul, it would have been unwise for him to brag about this title.

The sudden self-revelation of Christ, which consists of a combination of vision and audition, leaves the persecutor of Christians disoriented. Blinded by the heavenly light, Saul is left utterly helpless. The christophany "has the effect of *reducing Saul to nothingness.*"[3] "Saul is left in limbo," his identity is suspended, he is at the mercy of his traveling companions.[4] Without their support and guidance he would be totally lost. Whether the fact that Saul neither eats nor drinks for the next three days is a sign of physical distress or the beginning of repentance, which prepares him for his baptism, remains an open question. His identity has to be reshaped in a kind of *creatio ex nihilo.* He's at point zero. One thing is already certain: the Christians in Damascus are safe from him from now on. They don't have to fear this persecutor anymore. The problem, though, is that none of the Christians at Damascus know it! How could they? Thus, further information is needed—divine intervention must come.

While the blinded persecutor is on his way to Damascus to await further instructions there about his future (Acts 9:8), the focus of the narrative shifts to Ananias. He is a (Christian) disciple in the city (v. 10). In the narrative he will take on the role of a skeptic. He expresses all the possible doubts and fears about Saul. What could there be other than fear in the Christian community at Damascus concerning this man? Had Saul not been a threat to their lives? Why should they suddenly be willing to welcome this dangerous man? No one would be surprised if they all closed their doors and hid! This is the kind of atmosphere that Saul undoubtedly will be confronted with. Thus, the exalted Christ has to use his heavenly authority to mediate between the two enemy parties, the persecuted and the persecutor. But it is not that easy, for when he tells Ananias to go out and meet with Saul, Ananias is more than hesitant to carry out what the Lord commissions him to do. He reminds Jesus of Saul's evil plans (9:13-14).

By the way, keep in mind what this could mean for readers who are skeptical of the Christian Paul. How could this help them overcome their own possible doubts? This Saul/Paul is so utterly Jewish, from the very beginning at the feet of Gamaliel up to the very end in Rome. According to Luke, there is no difference in his Jewishness from his pre- to his post-conversion life. What makes all the difference in his identity, though, is the revelation of the exalted Christ near Damascus. This special experience of the risen Christ is, for Paul, the turning point in his life. Yet he always remains faithful to the God of Israel. Before his conversion he is completely loyal to the commandments of the Torah, and thus becomes so zealous that he persecutes the believers in Christ. After his conversion he proclaims the risen Christ as the fulfillment of the hope of Israel with exactly the same kind of commitment and earnestness.

The reigning skepticism about the Jewish persecutor Saul is overcome when Christ discloses his plan for Paul. He is a "chosen instrument of mine to carry my name before the Gentiles and the kings and the sons of Israel" (9:15). We must pay special attention to the word order here. The Gentiles come first! Paul is to bring the gospel primarily to the Gentiles. Israel comes second in his mission for Christ Jesus. (The word "kings" in verse 15 refers to Israel and not to the Roman Empire. Paul will actually have to defend his gospel in Acts 26 before King Agrippa.) This is important news for us as readers. We expect Paul to carry out this missionary program, first to the Gentiles and then to Israel. But we will see that it's going to be just the other way around.

Paul will start his missionary program in the synagogues of Damascus (v. 20)! This will always remain his missionary pattern: he goes first to Israel and then to the Gentiles (cf. Acts 13:46-48), from the beginning at Damascus to the very end in Rome, where he also meets only with the Jews of the city (Acts 28:17-28). Their divided reaction to his proclamation of Christ (vv. 23-24) *finally* makes him accept *fully* what he was sent out to do from the outset in Acts 9:15, namely, to be Christ's messenger primarily to the Gentile world (28:28). The overriding picture that we as readers will get, however, is of a Paul who, with great verve, tries to bring the name of Jesus to the Jews. Luke presents Paul as a failing missionary of Jesus to the Jews. Only twice does Luke report missionary efforts that concern Gentiles (Paul at Lystra in Acts 14:8-18, and Paul at Athens in 17:16-34), and both stories end with no great success (see Conclusion). Yet strangely, in the summaries, the success of the gospel in the Gentile world is emphasized (Acts 14:27; 15:12; 21:19). This is in conflict with the narrated facts, which concentrate almost exclusively on Jews as the audience for Paul's gospel preaching. However, this tension is no flaw in the narrative, but is purposefully designed to justify Paul. The narrated Paul has done as much as he possibly could to convince Jews about Jesus. Thus, if they reject his missionary efforts, they have failed, not Paul. Apparently it is a prerequisite for Paul to proclaim the gospel to Jews before his missionary way to the Gentiles is free. In other words: Paul has never given up on Israel. Rather, it's Israel that again and again gives up on Paul—even though what he proclaims is not something new, but the fulfillment of their long-awaited hope, the hope for resurrection that has been accomplished by Christ (Luke 2:25-32; Acts 28:20).

The programmatic prophecy in Acts 9:15-16 hints at the tragic outcome of Paul's missionary efforts. Paul must suffer for Christ. The sufferings he will have to face are not accidental, but part of the divine plan. Paul will be beaten up, imprisoned (Acts 16:19-23), and even stoned (14:19). He foresees tribulations and even his death (20:22-25). He will pay with his life for the sake of Christ. Even though this portrait of Paul cannot be called a theology of the cross, it certainly is not to be equated with a so-called theology of glory, of which, for example, Käsemann has accused Luke.[5] Luke's portrait of Paul is not a heroic glorification. Instead, it presents his martyrdom as being for Christ's sake. Whereas Paul himself preaches "Christ crucified" (1 Cor. 1:23), Luke portrays a Paul in agony for Christ.

First, however, his initial agony for the sake of Christ must come to an end. Ananias has good news for Saul. The time of physical and mental blindness shall be over. Saul will no longer be reduced to nothingness; the reshaping of his identity has begun, and this identity will make him a follower of Christ. His life has been completely turned around; he is transformed from persecutor to proclaimer of Christ. Blessed by one of his former enemies, he regains his sight when the blindness falls like scales from his eyes. Filled with the Holy Spirit, he is ready to be baptized. He takes food again and is strengthened. In other words, his identity formation is complete. He's back on the road, but how does he know what to do now? We hear of no instruction from Ananias. Wouldn't it be his duty to tell Paul what Christ had told him, that Paul is "to carry my name before the Gentiles and the kings and the sons of Israel" (9:15)? We can't simply assume this. Luke could have told the story some other way. Important issues are often dealt with in retelling them a second or even third time. Luke does this with Paul's conversion, which he narrates three times (Acts 9; 22; 26). He also does this with the apostolic decree (Acts 15:20, 29; 21:25).

Even Peter has to retell his encounter with Cornelius when he returns to Jerusalem (Acts 11:18). Retelling is part of Luke's narrative strategy for educating his readers. When he chooses a different strategy, as in Acts 9:15, this also has a reason. If Paul was aware of the pattern of his mission—first and foremost to the Gentiles and only second to Israel—then he should have begun by finding a Gentile audience. Instead, he goes "immediately" (v. 20) to the synagogues of the city. This will always remain Paul's strategy, and the narrator will take us up to Jerusalem, where Paul eventually is arrested in the temple as we learn that the exalted Christ had at least hinted at the Gentile mission in Damascus (Acts 22:15: "to all persons"; Greek: *pros pantas anthropous*). It had become all the more clear—according to Paul's own witness—when he left Damascus and returned to Jerusalem, where Christ commanded him in the temple, "Go, for I will send you far away to the Gentiles" (22:21). Paul is called to a mission among Gentiles, and there is no doubt about it—even Paul is aware of it. That's good for us to know. But why then, if it violates his commission, is Paul preoccupied with preaching Christ to Israel? One reason is that Luke is able to stress the Jewishness of his narrated Paul. Paul tries everything possible to reach out to the synagogues, to win Jews for Christ. The other reason is that, according to Luke's narrative strategy, it is Peter and not Paul who opens up the gates to proclaim Christ to the Gentile world in Acts 10 (see chapter 6).

Thus, for Paul, any contact with the Gentile world is prohibited, at least for the time being, until Peter appears on the scene again to meet with Cornelius. By the way, this also explains the somewhat strange order of the narrative. Paul's conversion story seems to be out of place. It appears between the first ethnic border crossing of the gospel (the Ethiopian eunuch, Acts 8:26-40) and Peter's encounter with Cornelius (Acts 10). Yes, Paul is going to be a missionary to the Gentiles, but this ethnic door has not been opened yet. Paul will have to wait until Peter's time has come. Even then the focus of Paul's missionary efforts in the Lukan narrative will always remain on the synagogues.

For now, we readers who can't anticipate the developing story line are a bit puzzled because Paul does not seem to do what he is told to do. He enters into the synagogues of Damascus and "immediately" proclaims Jesus as the Son of God (Acts 9:20). What a quick study! Now he proclaims Jesus with the same kind of vigor that he had when he persecuted him and his followers. Whatever Paul does, he does with all his being. There is no compromise for Paul, and this character trait will get him into trouble. This side of his personality sounds familiar. His enemies become his friends, and his friends, enemies. What a mess! "Is not this the man who destroyed those in Jerusalem who called upon this [Jesus'] name?" But Paul seems to love confusion. The more the Jews become confused, the more Paul steps up his missionary efforts to prove "that Jesus is the Christ" (9:22). This, of course, is not met with approval or praise, but with the opposite. "The Jews" plot to kill him (9:23). For the first time in Acts, the narrator uses the generalized term the Jews' with a solely negative connotation. Of course, only the Jews of Damascus are meant, but this generalization is still striking. The tone sharpens and hostility is on the rise. It's interesting that this polemical undertone becomes more strident as Paul, the Jewish missionary for Christ, appears on the scene. Again, it shows that Luke is not a distant observer and narrator, but clearly takes sides—and it becomes obvious that he feels especially close to Paul.

Paul the persecutor becomes the persecuted. He fears for his life, but with the help of his new friends he is able to escape (v. 25). In Jerusalem it's the same game again: Paul causes total confusion. Who can make sense of this man? First he persecuted Christ and his followers, now he proclaims him. At this point, Barnabas (first introduced in Acts 4:36) intervenes. His information about Paul's conversion convinces the Christian community, except for the Hellenists (the Greek-speaking Jewish Christians from the Diaspora) with whom Paul argues. What they argue about is not said, but one can infer that it must have addressed the question of how to include the Gentiles in the preaching of the gospel. The Hellenists historically took the position that circumcision is not required as a prerequisite for baptism, which, by the way, will also be the position that the Lukan Peter will eventually take in Acts 10 (see chapter 6). In this respect, then, even Peter would have to be put theologically on the side of the Hellenists—which is contrary to Luke's own narrative portrayal of Peter.

At any rate, if the Hellenists were more open to the inclusion of Gentiles, as it may be historically assumed, then Paul's opposition to them means that he resists an opening of the gates to the Gentile world in the proclamation of Christ. It is noteworthy that this opposition is an intra-Christian one, but Paul causes trouble outside and inside the Christian community. Both opposition groups, the one at Damascus (9:23-24) and the one at Jerusalem (v. 29), want to kill him. Thus, only one solution is possible: send Paul back to Tarsus, as far away as possible! What a relief for all the participants! Sure enough, just after Paul leaves, peace arrives. This is not only the kind of peace that accompanies the success of the gospel, it's also the kind of peace one experiences when a problem has been solved. Paul, the troublemaker, is gone. Where there is no Paul, there is peace.

HOMILETIC POSSIBILITIES FOR THE PERSECUTED PERSECUTOR: THE CONVERSION OF PAUL

The conversion of Paul poses some interesting problems for preaching. The rather extended narrative unit requires some careful homiletical planning. Following the exegesis above, we're dealing with a nonheroic narrative. Paul is not glorified as a hero. But God's work of grace, even to Gentiles, continues anyway. We'll follow the Lukan narrative theology as it emerges through the exegetical sections outlined above.

Introduction
Saul the persecutor meets Christ the persecuted on the Damascus road.

With this introduction, preachers need only set the scene. Perhaps a description of Michelangelo's famous painting would do.

> Michelangelo's painting of St. Paul's conversion offers a startling sight. Above is Christ, looming in the clouds. Just as ominously, Saul is pictured below. He's lying on the ground with his arm raised, as if shielding himself. Of course, the painting shouldn't surprise us. This meeting of the risen Christ with Saul the persecutor is not some sweet "How I Found Jesus" story. The picture shows it well. Jesus has found Saul—and Saul has been blinded and knocked to the ground.

Scene 1
Now Saul finds himself in need of divine help.

With this first scene, the preacher has the opportunity to picture Saul reduced to "nothingness," as our exegete has eloquently put it. Up to this point, Acts offers a narration of *Saul's* actions: holding coats at Stephen's stoning, or getting letters to carry out persecutions, then following through, with deadly consequences.

Preachers would be wise not to pass over Saul's helplessness too quickly here. Saul is not just an ordinary guy who is slowed down by disease. No, Saul is a man of action who now can do nothing. He is utterly helpless. If there is any way out of this mess, it's not through self-help books or by pulling a little harder on his own bootstraps. Saul needs help beyond himself—*divine* help. That's why he does what the voice tells him: "Rise and enter the city, and you will be told what you are to do." How unlike the persecutor with the resume to die for! Saul is at the mercy of the Christ he met on the road, and needs help from here on out.

Scene 2
So how does Christ help? By calling an old enemy to heal him: Ananias.

Isn't this just like God? We enjoy stories about ordinary people like us who, well, like us and do nice things for us. That's why we read *Reader's Digest* and listen to Paul Harvey's "The Rest of the Story" pieces on the radio. God in Christ, however, works through a different logic. If Saul needs healing, Christ will send one of the very people Saul had been persecuting, Ananias.

> The idea from Saul's point of view is almost comic. Imagine you are sitting in the dentist's office. You have one of those killer toothaches and something must be done about it. Oh, the hygienist is as helpful as can be. He politely helps you into the chair, gently puts on the goggles, and leaves you lying there listening to "The Girl from Ipanema" playing over the office speakers. But then, just when you're getting comfortable with the idea of having your tender tooth worked on, the dentist walks in. And surprise—it's a guy you knew from junior high, the one that you and your friends teased mercilessly. Wouldn't you know it? Just at the moment you're most vulnerable and in pain, a person is sent to heal you who may still be nursing an old grudge. As much as you look forward to relief from the toothache, this is decidedly not good news. Saul would understand. He is blind, hungry, and thirsty, and waiting for God's instruction—whatever it is—when God calls an old enemy to heal him.

Scene 3
Of course, Ananias doesn't like Christ's idea, either.

Here the preacher explores the other side of the odd moment facilitated by Christ's Damascus road appearance to Saul. Again, preachers should not be dismissive here. These two were not enemies who didn't know each other. Ananias even mentions Saul's reputation to the Lord in a vision—as if Christ might not have been reading the local papers! Indeed, what is ironic with Saul is truly tragic for Ananias. As part of a community suffering persecution, he senses real, bona fide risk here. Since the sermon proceeds to deal with the notion of enemies and reconciliation, preachers would be wise to take Ananias's objections with utmost seriousness. One might even try to come up with contemporary examples of persecuted and oppressed people, and imagine them going to heal their persecutors and oppressors. It's one tall order.

Scene 4
So Christ teaches Ananias about Saul's call: he will suffer in his mission to the Gentiles.

So what does the Lord do? How does Christ persuade Ananias that this is the right idea? Perhaps by moving through the options, we can bridge the gap between the Lord's announcement of Saul's mission and Ananias's surprising consent to heal him.

> The text is sparse here. What we have is the Lord's announcement of Saul's mission and Ananias's response. The Lord says, "Go, for he is a chosen instrument of mine to carry my name before the Gentiles and the kings and the sons [children] of Israel; for I myself will show him how much he must suffer for the sake of my name." Then, having heard this, Ananias goes and does what he says he didn't want to do! Why? Well, perhaps Ananias thought this mission to the Gentiles was a good idea. Who, after all, is against sending missionaries? Ananias may have thought this, but that is not

sufficient to explain why he would have gone. The Lord, after all, wasn't asking him to visit a friendly missionary just returned from overseas, but a persecutor of the church. So maybe, just maybe, the key is in the second half of the Lord's announcement: "I myself will show him how much he must suffer. . . ." Now that word must have caught Ananias's ears: suffering! That's just what Saul needs! But hold it—we're not talking about malicious glee here. Ananias doesn't respond just because he looks forward to Saul's pain. No, there is probably something deeper than that going on. If the Lord commissions Saul, it is a commission to serve the community of the suffering. And that's a vocation that Ananias understands.

Scene 5
Now Saul can be blessed through the touch of his enemy.

Preachers can now picture the scene in which the scales fall from Saul's eyes. Please note, however, that the scene is not one of unadulterated happiness. Saul is indeed healed, but the tragic brokenness, the failure, and the suffering continue. He is blessed, all right, but to be blessed through the touch of an enemy is not to be healed lightly. There are no group hugs; there is just the dirty business of ongoing reconciliation in the face of struggle, confrontation, and yes, even failure. What does this look like? Preachers may wish to review some of the articles about the Truth and Reconciliation Commission in South Africa. As a requirement for amnesty, those who engaged in violent acts during the apartheid era had to tell all. They had to confess what they had done and face the very people they had wronged. Sure, we think it sounds like they were "getting off the hook." Perhaps on one level they were. Nonetheless, the exchanges witnessed before the Commission in South Africa are not for the fainthearted. They are part of the real, ongoing work of reconciliation. No doubt Saul would understand. In his mission to the Gentiles and in his suffering for it, Saul comes face to face with the inscrutable grace of God. This grace is costly for those whom it calls. For those of us on this side of the Jewish-Christian divide, it comes no more easily. If we are healed, it is a healing directed toward suf-

fering that begins with a realization of Christian complicity in Jewish persecution. How did one commentator react to Pope John Paul II's placement of his prayer for forgiveness in a crack of the Wailing Wall in Jerusalem? "Well, it's a start." So it is with God's unfathomable healing. It is a gracious call that leads into the heart of suffering. That's what happens when you're blessed by an enemy.

Conclusion

Strange, isn't it? You never quite know whom you'll meet on the road. Just ask Saul. The Christ he met there called him from the work of inflicting pain to the grace of struggling through it for the sake of the gospel. Oh, it may not be the way to success. But it is the way to Damascus—and beyond.

CHAPTER SIX

Divine Matching: The Breakthrough of the Gospel into the Gentile World *or* The Conversion of Peter

Acts 10:1-11:18

Lectionary: Year A, Baptism of the Lord
Years A, B, and C, Easter (alternative)
Year B, Sixth Sunday of Easter
Year C, Fifth Sunday of Easter

TEXT

[1]There was a man at Caesarea named Cornelius, a centurion of the so-called Italian Cohort, [2]a devout man who feared God along with all his household, gave alms liberally to the people, and prayed constantly to God. [3]About the ninth hour of the day he saw clearly an angel of God coming in and saying to him, "Cornelius!" [4]He stared at him, and being frightened he said, "What is it, Lord?" And he said to him, "Your prayers and your alms have ascended as a memorial offering before God. [5]And now send men to Joppa, and bring one Simon who is called Peter; [6]he is lodging with Simon, a tanner, whose house is by the seaside." [7]When the angel who spoke to him had departed, he called two of his servants and a devout soldier from among those that waited on him, [8]and having related everything to them, he sent them to Joppa.

[9]The next day, as they were on their journey and approaching the city, Peter went up on the roof terrace to pray at about the sixth hour of the day. [10]And he became hungry and desired something to eat; but while they were preparing food, he fell into an ecstasy.

[11]He saw the heaven opened, and a vessel came down, resembling a great linen, being lowered to the ground by its four corners. [12]In it were all kinds of four-legged creatures and reptiles of the earth and birds of the sky. [13]And a voice said to him, "Rise, Peter, slaughter and eat!" [14]But Peter said, "Never, Lord; for I have never eaten anything common and unclean!" [15]And the voice said to him again, for a second time, "What God has cleansed, you must not call common!" [16]This happened three times, and the vessel was taken up at once into heaven.

[17]Now while Peter was still trying to make sense out of the vision he had seen, behold, the men sent by Cornelius, inquiring after the house of Simon, arrived at the gate. [18]They called out to ask whether Simon who was called Peter was lodging there. [19]And while Peter was still pondering the vision, the Spirit said to him, "Behold, three men are here, looking for you. [20]So rise and go down, and go along with them without hesitation; for I have sent them." [21]And Peter went down to the men and said, "Behold, I am the one you are looking for. What is the reason for your coming?" [22]And they said, "Cornelius, a centurion, an upright and God-fearing man who is well spoken of among all the Jewish people, was instructed by a holy angel to send for you to come to his house, and to hear what you have to say." [23]So he called them in and treated them as his guests.

The next day he got up and went off with them, and some of the brethren from Joppa went with them. [24]And on the following day they arrived in Caesarea. Cornelius was expecting them and had called in his kinsmen and close friends. [25]As Peter was about to enter, Cornelius went to meet him, fell down at his feet, and worshiped him. [26]But Peter lifted him up, saying, "Stand up; I too am only a human being." [27]And talking with him, he went in and found many persons gathered there. [28]He said to them, "You yourselves know that it is unlawful for a Jew to associate with or visit a Gentile; but God has shown me that no one should call a human being common or unclean. [29]So when I was sent for, I came without objection. May I ask, then, why you sent for me?" [30]And Cornelius said, "Four days ago, about this hour, I was keeping the ninth hour of prayer in my house, and behold, a man robed in bright clothes stood before me. [31]He said to me, 'Cornelius, your prayer has been heard and your alms have been remembered before God. [32]Send therefore to Joppa and ask for Simon who is called Peter; he is lodging in the house of Simon, a tanner, by the sea.' [33]So I sent for you at once, and you have been kind enough to come. Now then, we are all present before God to hear all that you have been commanded by the Lord." [34]And Peter opened his mouth and said, "Truly I realize now that God shows no partiality, [35]but in every nation anyone who fears him and does what is upright is acceptable to him. [36]You know the word which he sent to the children of Israel, proclaiming the gospel of peace through Jesus Christ—he is Lord of all—[37]the word which was proclaimed throughout Judea, beginning from Galilee after the baptism which John preached: [38]Jesus of Nazareth, how God anointed him with the Holy Spirit and power; how he went about doing good and healing all who were in the power of the devil, because God was with him. [39]And we are witnesses of all that he did both in the country of the Jews and in Jerusalem; they put him to death by hanging him on a piece of wood. [40]This man God raised up on the third day and made him manifest, [41]not to all the people, but to us, witnesses chosen by God beforehand, who ate and drank with him after he rose from the dead. [42]And he commanded us to preach to the people, and to testify that he is the one appointed by God to be judge of the living and the dead. [43]To him all the prophets bear witness that everyone who believes in him receives forgiveness of sins through his name."

[44]While Peter was still saying these things, the Holy Spirit came down upon all who were listening to the word. [45]And the believers from among the circumcised who came with Peter were bewildered, because the gift of the Holy Spirit had been poured out on the Gentiles, too. [46]For they heard them speaking in tongues and extolling God. Then Peter said, [47]"Can anyone withhold the water to baptize these people who have received the Holy Spirit just as we have?" [48]And he ordered them to be baptized in the name of Jesus Christ. They then asked him to stay for a couple of days.

Chapter 11

[1]Now the apostles and the brethren who were in Judea heard that the Gentiles also had welcomed the word of God. [2]So when Peter

came up to Jerusalem, circumcised believers attacked him, [3]saying, "You entered the house of uncircumcised people and ate with them." [4]Peter began to explain everything to them, step by step: [5]"I was in the town of Joppa praying, when in an ecstasy I had a vision. I saw a vessel resembling a great linen descending, being lowered from heaven by its four corners, and it came down to me. [6]Looking at it closely I could see and make out four-legged creatures of the earth, wild beasts, and birds of the air. [7]I also heard a voice say to me, 'Rise, Peter, slaughter and eat!' [8]But I said, 'Never, Lord! For nothing common or unclean has ever entered my mouth!' [9]But the voice from heaven spoke out a second time, 'What God has cleansed, you must not call common!' [10]This happened three times, and all was drawn up again into heaven. [11]And behold, that very moment three men sent to me from Caesarea arrived at the house in which we were. [12]The Spirit told me to go with them without hesitation. These six brethren were with me, and we entered that man's house. [13]He informed us how he had seen the angel standing in his house saying, 'Send someone to Joppa and bring Simon, who is called Peter. [14]He will say to you words by which you and all your household will be saved.' [15]As I began to address them, the Holy Spirit came down upon them, just as it did on us in the beginning. [16]Then I remembered the word of the Lord, how he said, 'John baptized with water, but you will be baptized with the Holy Spirit.' [17]If then God gave them the same gift he gave us when we came to believe in the Lord Jesus Christ, who was I to be able to withstand God?" [18]When they heard this they were silenced. And they praised God, saying, "So God has granted repentance unto life to the Gentiles as well."

(Author's translation)

INTRODUCTION

This section contains four readings from the lectionary (10:25-34; 10:34-43; 10:44-48; 11:1-18), yet they are treated here as different parts of one consistent story. This is an example of a situation in which narrative exegesis must reject the oversegmentation of a given story. Granted, it would be impossible to explore the entire narrative of 10:1–11:18 sufficiently in one sermon. Yet in spite of treating one and a half chapters of Acts as a unit, we should still be able to produce results that will be a useful resource for preaching.

From a narrative methodology, that which applies in general to all of Luke-Acts also applies to the story about the encounter of Peter and Cornelius. Unless we read the Lukan narrative as a unified entity, we could miss the point of the plot. Its subtle structures and features—and, for that matter, its irony—could easily be overlooked. This is true in particular for Acts 10:1–11:18. On the surface of the text, we might wonder, for example, why the story is so long and parts have to be retold. But this is precisely part of the Lukan narrative strategy. We have observed it before in the Emmaus pericope (chapter 3) and in the conversion story of Paul (chapter 5): important aspects of the story have to be told more than once. This is not to bore but to educate the reader. In this case, the meeting of Peter and Cornelius is much more than just a private encounter. It is one of the highlights and key stories of the entire Lukan narrative!

Peter, or rather the Holy Spirit, accomplishes a major breakthrough of the gospel: it finally reaches the Gentiles. This may sound routine to those of us who are Christian insiders, but from a Jewish point of view we are Gentiles, and therefore there is an ethnic, cultural, and religious boundary between us and "them" (i.e., Jews like the Lukan Peter and Paul). Thus far, Luke has expended much effort to tell the story from a Jewish perspective; up to this point in the narrative, the Gentiles had to remain outsiders. Their hour has not yet come. But it has always been clear from the beginning of the story in Luke 2, Simeon's prophecy, that it will come. The salvation accomplished through Christ's resurrection also includes the Gentiles. Christ's salvation is for all humankind, for everyone who fears God, as we will learn in the Peter and Cornelius story. But Israel is and remains the source of this salvific act. Out of its midst has come the Messiah. Yet he is not only Israel's Messiah, but also the Savior of the entire world. Christ's salvation is universal. This has been made clear from the beginning of Luke's Gospel. Although the other three Gospels also deal—albeit differently—with the question of how to include the Gentiles in the gospel of Jesus Christ, Luke expends much more narratorial effort and narrative space to build up this historic moment.

Luke has been clear throughout his narrative that believers in Christ are firmly rooted within Judaism and its traditions. There is not a single issue on which Christ's believers depart from Jewish faith and traditions. On the contrary, faith in Christ is portrayed as the long-awaited hope of Israel, which means the hope for resurrection. This has been accomplished by Christ. He is the Exalted One who now sits at the right hand of God Almighty and who has begun to pour out the Holy Spirit to summon the (Jewish) people to the gospel (Acts 2:32-33). Christ, the fulfilled hope of Judaism, is Israel's contribution to the salvation of the world. This should make Israel rejoice and feel proud and honored (cf. Luke 2:29-32). Faith in Christ is not a new faith or a new religion, but stands in full accordance with Judaism. Therefore, Luke has made every possible effort to emphasize that the first believers in Christ in Jerusalem, the apostles, the so-called "Hebrews" and "Hellenists" (Acts 6:1), and all the other thousands, remain firmly rooted in Jewish traditions. Thus, they worship and pray in the temple, and just in case criticisms against this new Jewish group arise, Luke makes it clear that the accusations against Stephen are completely false (Acts 6:13-15). It is therefore tragic that, due to the stoning of Stephen, believers in Christ (with the exception of the apostles) are expelled from the city (Acts 8:1). On the other hand, because of this expulsion, the gospel spreads into regions beyond Jerusalem and Judea, namely, to Galilee (Acts 8), and eventually even proceeds into ethnic and cultural areas where the question of who is clean or unclean has to be dealt with. The Ethiopian eunuch is the first boundary dispute. In spite of his status as a castrated man, which would make it impossible for him to become a Jewish proselyte, he behaves like a God-fearing Gentile: he prays and worships in the temple, in the section reserved for non-Jews (Acts 8:27).[1] This God-fearing habit suffices for him to be baptized and to become a believer in Christ.

Including "boundary cases" like the Ethiopian eunuch within the growing and geographically spreading Christian community is to be welcomed, but this poses a fundamental theological and practical problem for the community of believers in Christ: how are they to relate to the commandments of the Torah? Up to this point the believers in Christ had always stayed firmly within the boundaries of Torah. Luke presents Peter in particular as a believer in Christ who strongly lives according to the rules and regulations of the Torah. This is exactly the reason he has difficulties in Joppa when he encounters the startling vision in which a voice from heaven compels him to "slaughter and eat" not only clean but also unclean—or common—animals (Acts 10:13-14). Peter has always behaved as a committed, faithful Jew. So this encounter must come as a surprise that confuses not only Peter but also the Lukan reader. Peter has been the perfect example of the symbiosis of Judaism and faith in Christ, but this image is shaken. Peter is shaken, and we, the readers, witness a disturbance in early Christian history. It marks a major threat to Christian identity. Nonetheless, something very important has to be solved: if faith in Christ is supposed to become a universally shared hope that is directed toward the Gentile world, then how are the Gentiles actually to be included? Do they have to become Jewish proselytes first (meaning circumcision before baptism)? The Christian stance toward Torah is under question, and this last issue of the Lukan concept of Christianity has to be resolved. Who is better suited to carry out this task than Peter, the utterly committed Jew who believes in Christ?

THE CONVERSION OF CORNELIUS OR THE CONVERSION OF PETER? THE NEED TO CORRECT A COMMON MISREADING

It is quite common to call the narrative about Peter's encounter with Cornelius the "conversion of Cornelius." Joseph A. Fitzmyer's commentary on Acts is but one example of this perception. He entitles his section on Acts 10:1–11:18, "Conversion of Cornelius and His Household in Caesarea."[2] But who is actually converted? There seems to be no justification in the text for calling this a conversion of Cornelius. If anyone is "converted" at all it's either God or Peter. If God, then it's because God has let it be known through an angel that Cornelius's prayers and alms "have ascended as a memorial offering before God" (10:4). Why and how this change is motivated we are not told. It's just part of God's plan. God must have had a change of mind or salvation history now simply takes a different course. However, this is not a matter of whimsy, because behind the new direction there is a plan in which God has begun to pair up, or "match," two opposites. The one person who has to be convinced, though, is Peter. Throughout the narrative, he is portrayed as the one who at first is opposed and then reluctant to cross cultural and religious boundaries. But he is not the active character in this story. The Spirit seems to be the true revolutionary, the one agent way ahead of Peter, who is himself slow to perceive and act. He has to be forced to carry out what God's Holy Spirit has in mind. Therefore, we could call this story "The Conversion of Peter," since he is the one who has to turn from the old way to the new. God's messengers on earth don't have an easy job. First it's Paul who is transformed from an enemy into an advocate of the Christian faith. Now an almost identical thing happens to Peter. The speed of the Holy Spirit leaves him speechless.

DIVINE MATCHING, STEP ONE: GOOD NEWS FOR CORNELIUS (10:1-8)

As a centurion, the commander of a hundred soldiers, Cornelius must have been a Roman citizen, and thus belonged to the elite. That Luke locates the story in Caesarea is not accidental, because the town, a seaport on the Mediterranean Sea where the Roman prefect or procurator resided, is a perfect place to inaugurate the mission to the Gentiles. It's far enough from—yet at the same time close enough to—Jerusalem and thus symbolizes the two sides of Judaism: its openness to Mediterranean culture and its commitment to the traditions of the past. Except for the fact that Palestine was occupied, one could compare Caesarea to Tel Aviv in our time.

Luke describes Cornelius in ways similar to his characterization of the centurion of Capernaum (Luke 7:1-10). Adding to the Matthean version of the story (Matt. 8:5-13), Luke notes that *Jews* tell Jesus that the centurion "loves our people, and it is he who built our synagogue for us" (Luke 7:5). Whereas the centurion of Capernaum donates a synagogue, the centurion of Caesarea gives alms "liberally" to Jews. They both are portrayed as patrons of

Jews and their institutions. Jews certainly do not have to suffer under any oppression from these Romans; rather, they benefit from them, as both are openly sympathetic to the Jews. What a joy and what an advantage for Jews to be under their legislative and military power! Doubtless Luke exaggerates here a bit. His positive stance toward Roman rule has been frequently noted.[3] First, in the centurion of Capernaum and in Cornelius, Luke creates ideal narrative figures through which he seeks to demonstrate that Christianity is no threat at all to Roman authority. Keep in mind that the first missionary success of Paul mentioned by name is the Roman proconsul of Cyprus, Sergius Paulus (Acts 13:4-12). What a sensation if this were historically true! Second, the profile of the two centurions is that of ideal non-Jewish sympathizers with Judaism. Cornelius in particular is portrayed as if he were a committed, faithful Jew. Luke calls him a "devout" and God-fearing person (Greek: *eusebes kai phoboumenos ton theon* [Acts 10:2]). According to Luke, to be a God-fearer means to honor, respect, and even worship the God of Israel, for Cornelius "prayed constantly to God" (v. 2).[4]

Fearing God had already been established as the decisive criterion for true worship and faith for all Israelites when Mary sang in her song of praise that God's "mercy is for those who fear him from generation to generation" (Greek: *tois phoboumenois auton* [Luke 1:50]). In their fear of the one and only, monotheistic God of Israel—in contrast to the worship of the many gods of the Greeks and the Romans (cf. Acts 14:8-18; 17:16-32; see next chapter)—both Jews and Gentiles are unified. What separates them, though, is the boundary that the commandments of the Torah require. God-fearing Gentiles are only obliged to keep certain regulations of the Torah, such as the ones outlined in the so-called apostolic decree in Acts 15:20, 29 and 21:25. The key difference between a God-fearing Gentile and a Jewish proselyte is circumcision (see Acts 15:5). A high Roman official such as Cornelius could not become a Jew because he had to remain loyal to the Roman emperor, who was seen as a god. He may have had no desire to become a Jew. Many lower-class people had an incentive to become Jews, and thus were circumcised, because of the synagogue "welfare system." Proselytes were regarded as full-fledged members with all the benefits and obligations of the synagogue community. Cornelius was a well-respected member of the Roman middle-class elite who did not suffer any financial or economic problems. As a God-fearer, he could show his sympathy to Judaism and yet remain a loyal Roman citizen.

These aspects of Cornelius are important for getting a proper understanding of the narrated event to come. Cornelius is not suffering, nor in despair. He is not out to change his life; rather, it is God's attitude toward a God-fearing Gentile that has changed. This is the key to fathoming the divine announcement, "Your prayers and your alms have ascended as a memorial offering before God" (Acts 10:4). The expression "memorial offering" is a technical term taken from HB sacrifices.[5] Still, the meaning of this announcement remains somewhat mysterious. Only by following the narrative to its end will the reader, like Cornelius, begin to fully understand its significance. "Memorial offering" actually will mean the recognition of God-fearing Gentiles as equals to Jewish (Christian) believers, though this is not fully disclosed yet.

Cornelius is being told to send for a certain "Simon who is called Peter" (Acts 10:5). The instructions about where to go and how to find this Simon Peter are precise and accurate. Being a devout God-fearing Gentile, Cornelius follows the divine command: at once he sends his servants and personal soldiers to Joppa to summon Peter to his house.

DIVINE MATCHING, STEP TWO: PETER OFF GUARD AND OFF TRACK (10:9-16)

Peter does not know yet what the next few days will bring. His life will pass through the center of a storm; there will be rough seas ahead. Peter will lose control, become utterly confused and lost, and his concept of Judaism will be shaken. Up to this point, it has always been clear that Christ Jesus is the fulfillment of Israel's long-awaited hope for salvation. Of course the Gentiles are to be addressed by and with the gospel, and they are to be included in the community of believers in Christ. But *how*? Well, Peter would have been in total agreement with what the pharisaic Christian believers will claim before the apostolic meeting at Jerusalem: "It is necessary for them to be circumcised and ordered to keep the law of Moses" (Acts 15:5). First comes circumcision, then baptism. After all, this is exactly the way it had been working for the Jewish believers in Christ. Peter is by no means a revolutionary who is agitating for nonkosher new ways. Under no circumstances does he want to be identified with any kind of apostasy from Judaism; rather, he sees himself as a devout, faithful Jewish Christian believer. Let Cornelius's messengers come and Peter will show them the Jewish way to God's salvation.

While Cornelius's men are on their way to Joppa, Peter is about to go up to the roof terrace for his morning prayer. He's a bit late today, for it's already about the sixth hour, which means it's around noontime. This is not the ordinary time for Jewish prayer; thus it must be his first prayer of the morning. This is a bit confusing because Peter has always been portrayed as being utterly committed to Jewish religious faith and practice. Moreover, we haven't even dealt with *where* Peter is staying. Luke, the author, is an impressively skillful narrator. He knows how to place important information that is easily overlooked on first reading. Those who divided the NT writings first into chapters and later into verses have thereby contributed immensely to directing readers toward a certain understanding of the writings. These reading devices can be helpful, but sometimes also misleading. When we look up Acts 10 in our Bibles, we think that a new subject begins with verse one. In this case it's true, and yet it's not, because the last verses of chapter 9 are not to be neglected, especially 9:43 (see 10:6, 32), which tells us that Peter was staying in Joppa at the house of a certain Simon, a tanner! This Simon was most likely a Jew, because it would be even more startling if "our" Simon Peter had entered the house of a Gentile. The fact that Peter socializes with a tanner is surprising news after all that has been said about him so far. Why does Peter lodge with such a man? A tanner, whose profession involves working on different sorts of animal skin and leather, inevitably comes into contact with blood. Thus, Peter is in danger of violating the purity laws of Torah. What a threat to his Jewish identity! At the very least, a tanner is not the kind of person one associates with if one wants to come across as a devout, practicing Jew. So what makes Simon Peter begin to change his mind and attitude? This is strange, very strange—what's going on here?

Beyond this, Peter is also late for his morning prayer. Peter is off the track of pious virtue—he is no longer the kind of person the reader can easily identify with. Since Peter is late this morning, he hasn't had anything to eat yet. The people of the household are preparing food for lunch, but Peter does his duty, goes up to the roof terrace, and gets ready for prayer, meanwhile smelling the odors of food. Granted, Luke is not very interested in a psychological profile of Peter. This is not a case study about Peter in need, yet the narrator clearly hints at the humanity of the situation. People who don't eat are hungry and are therefore naturally tempted when they smell food. Luke is a brilliant narrator who does not make a big fuss over this detail, but it's clear that the human condition plays a large part in this divine matching story.

Peter must be very hungry, for he falls into an ecstasy, and in his trance he experiences a strange vision—almost as if it were a kind of heavenly punishment as well as sweet revenge for being late this morning. The confusing thing about the different kinds of animals that he sees in the vessel, which descends in the form of a linen, is that it contains a mixture of clean and unclean animals (the "reptiles of the earth"—Greek: *herpeta tes ges* [v. 12]— are regarded as particularly unclean).[6] To follow the heavenly voice's command, "Slaughter and eat!" would be a violation of Jewish purity regulations, and thus must be distressing to Peter. What does he do with such a divine command? Peter is strong in his Jewish faith, and thus able to withstand this advice to apostatize. But the voice from heaven is stubborn and does not give up on Peter. Three times it repeats its command to betray Jewish custom and traditions. Peter still resists this order to commit apostasy, but he is bewildered. After all, who is he to reject this divine command? "What God has cleansed, you must not call common!" (10:15). This definitely involves a dramatic, radical change of the meaning of the Jewish purity laws, and thus of Torah as such. The consequences of this change are not yet fully known to Peter or to us readers. With regard to Peter, he is—not unlike Saul in his conversion encounter with Christ—also left in a state of limbo.

There are two complementary visions, one to Cornelius and one to Peter, but neither man really knows what is going on. It's still a kind of mystery. But God's Holy Spirit is moving ahead. Biblical stories contain suspenseful moments and this is one of them.

DIVINE MATCHING, STEP THREE: HOW TO GET PETER GOING (10:17-23*a*)

This is a kind of interim story that functions to bridge the two different visions. As isolated events, the visions of Cornelius and Peter don't seem to make much sense, but put together as bits and pieces of a larger divine puzzle, they reveal God's plan to bring Jews and Gentiles together. While Peter is still shocked and bewildered, the men sent by Cornelius arrive. Now the Spirit gets actively involved by commanding Peter to welcome the men and to go with them to Caesarea, for "I have sent them" (10:20). It is important for Peter to know that God's Holy Spirit is the divine agent behind these disturbing events; this realization is reinforced by what the strangers have to say about Cornelius and his vision. Again, it is stressed that Cornelius is an "upright and God-fearing man who is well spoken of among all the Jewish people" (v. 22). This makes him an ideal recipient of the (Jewish) Christian gospel. Being led by the Spirit, Peter feels secure and welcomes the strangers into the house.

DIVINE MATCHING, STEP FOUR: A NEW FUNDAMENTAL INSIGHT: PETER'S TESTIMONY ABOUT GOD'S IMPARTIALITY (10:23*b*-43)

Peter is about to regain control of the situation—at least in part. He knows what he has to do next: go to Caesarea and look for Cornelius. He takes a few of his fellow Jewish Christians along with him; in Acts 11:12 we learn there are six. Upon Peter's arrival in Caesarea, Cornelius falls at his feet, which from a person of his position and rank is definitely an unusual gesture of high esteem toward a Jew. It shows his great respect for this heaven-sent person. However, in the eyes of a Jew, this gesture could be misunderstood as treating a human being as an object of worship (cf. the temptation story [Luke 4:8] and Paul and Barnabas at Lystra [Acts 14:8-18]), and such an apotheosis would be blasphemy. Peter's answer—"Stand up; I too am only a human being" (10:26)—accomplishes two things: first, it secures and reaffirms the fundamental values of Jewish monotheism, and second, it demonstrates that Peter regards the Gentile centurion as an equal. This equality did not necessarily have to be acknowledged, as Paul makes clear when he boasts about his Jewish identity and background (Phil. 3:4-6; cf. Rom. 1:16).

For Peter to view a God-fearing Gentile centurion as an equal is a first and major step forward toward a cross-cultural acceptance of Jews and Gentiles alike as members of the same family of God. Peter seems to get the point, but does he really get it yet? Is he aware of all the implications? When he enters the house of Cornelius, he feels obliged to remind his host that normally it would be unlawful for a Jew to socialize with a Gentile (Acts 10:28), for this inevitably risks the possibility of violating the purity laws. Doing business with Gentiles is one thing, but entering the house of a Gentile in private is a different question. Peter is willing to take this risk because God's Spirit is pushing and encouraging him: "God has shown me that no one should call a human being common or unclean" (v. 28). Peter begins to understand that his vision on the roof terrace was not only about kosher and non-kosher food, but also people. Dietary laws in particular set a boundary between Jews and Gentiles that was not to be crossed. NT scholar Philip F. Esler remarks that

> although Jews were happy to mix with Gentiles in synagogues or possibly even in market-places or streets, eating with them was a very different matter. Eating was an occasion fraught with the possibility of breaching the purity code, one of the most crucial aspects of the Mosaic law for the maintenance of the separate identity of the Jewish *ethnos*. The antipathy of Jews towards table-fellowship with Gentiles, in the full sense of sitting around a table with them and sharing the same food, wine and vessels, was an intrinsic feature of Jewish life.[7]

Gentiles who respected Jewish law abstained from those things that offended Jews in particular (cf. the apostolic decree in Acts

15:20, 29 and 21:25). Cornelius is a God-fearing Gentile and thus especially sensitive about these issues that are crucial for any devout Jew. But still, Peter's insight marks a major turning point in his career as a Jewish apostle and missionary for Christ. If the clear-cut boundary between clean and unclean suddenly evaporates, then what's the use of Torah? What's the use of circumcision? What's the use of the dietary laws?

Maybe Peter is not fully aware of all the implications that inevitably follow from what he has just declared. At any rate, this seems to be shocking news, and so it is reassuring when Cornelius tells his part of the story, his experience of this vision (10:30-33). Of course, we know how it goes, but it's helpful to hear the story all over again from its beginning. It helps Peter (and of course the readers) to feel reassured that all that has been happening is "kosher," that it's part of God's salvific plan. After all, this is so new and will revolutionize the concept of God's people so much that it's good to hear it repeated. Then the seemingly disparate bits and pieces of this divine riddle become clearer and Peter feels increasingly confident: "Truly I realize now that God shows no partiality, but in every nation anyone who fears him and does what is upright is acceptable to him" (vv. 34-35). This is the key sentence in this whole chapter. Fearing God is the one and only decisive criterion for obtaining access to the God of Israel who is also the father of Jesus Christ. Mary's melodic proclamation that God's "mercy is for those who fear him from generation to generation" (Luke 1:50; see this chapter, above) has now also been declared to the Gentiles. It is no longer the law of Moses that defines who belongs and who does not belong to the people of God; rather, it is the fear of God that determines membership among God's people. This declaration depends on the salvific act of Christ—his life, death and resurrection—that is Israel's hope for all humankind. That salvation in Christ is to be addressed universally has been clear from the beginning of Luke-Acts (the Simeon canticle in Luke 2:29-32), but now it has become true for the Gentiles.

Peter's speech may well be his usual missionary sermon, his standard sermon for this occasion, but this is the first Christian sermon addressed to a Gentile audience. It is a summary of what has been preached about Jesus before, beginning with Israel as first and prime addressee (v. 36) and ending by declaring that "everyone who believes in him [Christ] receives forgiveness of sins through his name" (v. 43). This is almost identical to what Peter proclaimed at the Jewish Pentecost in Jerusalem when he quoted from the book of Joel and affirmed that "whoever calls on the name of the Lord shall be saved" (Joel 2:32 in Acts 2:21). The announcement has now reached the God-fearing Gentile world, leaving one important question: how will God's Spirit sanctify this newly established faith community? According to Peter himself, who quoted Joel at the first Jewish Pentecost, God's Spirit will be poured out on "all flesh" (Joel 2:28 in Acts 2:17). In the case of Cornelius, this is still to happen. But when? And under what conditions?

DIVINE MATCHING, STEP FIVE: WHAT A SURPRISE: IT'S PENTECOST AGAIN— THE PENTECOST OF THE GENTILES (10:44-48)

This section requires a careful comparative reading. Something unique is happening here. Keep in mind that Peter has always been in control of the Holy Spirit. Maybe that's pushing the point too far, but Peter thus far has appeared to have a kind of joint venture with the Spirit. At the first Pentecost, Peter declared that the outpouring of the Spirit is the gift that follows baptism: "Repent, and be baptized every one of you in the name of Jesus Christ for the forgiveness of your sins; and you shall receive the gift of the Holy Spirit" (Acts 2:38). Then in the Samaria mission, Luke explained why the Jerusalem apostles, Simon Peter and John, had to finish what Philip had begun. Philip had proclaimed the gospel and even baptized, but the Holy Spirit had not been poured out yet. For this to happen, the presence of the Jerusalem church authorities was required. Therefore, they sent Peter and John to Samaria to make the missionary project complete (Acts 8:14-17). Once hands were laid on the Samaritans who were present, they received the Holy Spirit (v. 17). It seems that the outpouring of the Spirit was bound to the presence of the Jerusalem apostles. Of course, this is the narrative perspective of Luke who, in the first half of Acts up to the apostolic council meeting, seeks to demonstrate the predominance of the twelve apostles and the Jerusalem church in general over against the so-called Hellenists and the Antioch church with its leading figures, Barnabas and Paul.

With this in mind, it is all the more striking to read what happens at Cornelius's house while Peter is delivering his standard sermon. He hasn't even finished when the Holy Spirit appears and, to the amazement of the Jewish Christians present, falls on *all* (Greek: *epi pantas*) who are there (10:44), even the Gentiles (v. 45). For Gentiles to be blessed by God's Holy Spirit and enabled to speak in tongues (v. 46) is unheard of and completely new. This must be a second Pentecost, the Pentecost for the Gentiles!

The surprise of Peter and his Jewish Christian friends is in itself somewhat surprising, because according to what has been narrated so far, Peter must have suspected what would happen. The outpouring of the Spirit should not have come as a surprise; it is an endorsement of what has become apparent, namely, that God-fearing Gentiles (not heathens!) have gained full access to God's family along with the Israelites. Still, Peter seems shocked and confused—and perhaps with some justification! After all, this presents a major difficulty for a devout Jew who has become an equally devout believer in Christ. Peter is caught in the middle of a deep conflict of loyalty: what is he to believe and follow? The word of God according to the Torah? Or the word of God according to the Holy Spirit?

If he follows the Torah, then he can no longer socialize with Gentiles and eat with them! He will have to face precisely this criticism from the other apostles upon his return to Jerusalem: "You entered the house of uncircumcised people and ate with them" (11:3). Peter is about to violate the dietary laws of the Torah, and thereby deny the necessary and salvific boundaries of Torah as a whole. Dietary laws are no *adiaphoron*, no matter of indifference, to a devout Jew!

But if Peter follows the word of God according to the Holy Spirit, he will be departing from Judaism and entering wholly new territory. There is no basis for this in the Torah, no scriptural reading that could help him out here. He is caught between two revelations, two exclusive models of salvation, and one cannot be harmonized with the other. Nevertheless, Luke will discern a solution, a kind of compromise, which he will demonstrate at the apostolic council in Acts 15. There it will become clear that for Luke, Gentile Christians will have to keep some of the commandments of the Torah—specifically, those that God-fearing Gentiles were to keep if they wanted to associate with Jews. The four commandments of the so-called apostolic decree (Acts 15:20, 29 and 21:25) seemingly were in practice in the community Luke addresses.[8]

Peter has to make a decision, and it will be a breathtaking one. He opts for the Holy Spirit: "Can anyone withhold the water to baptize these people who have received the Holy Spirit just as we have?" (10:47). The simple answer is: No! Thus he orders them to be baptized, and he and his companions agree to stay as guests at Cornelius's house, the first house church of Jewish and Gentile Christians! In fact, this will be the only one that is narrated in all of Luke-Acts (except for the summary remarks about the Antioch church in chapter 11:19-26). What has just happened is an historic moment. For Luke, it's crucial that it is Peter who becomes the one to accomplish this major breakthrough. Paul's authority would not have been strong enough to accomplish what Peter successfully does. Peter was needed to cross the bridge and close the gap between Jews and Gentiles. Remember how long it took Peter to fully comprehend and accept the means and ways of the Holy Spirit. The divine puzzle has finally been put together.

THE INCLUSION OF THE GENTILES AS CHALLENGE AND THREAT: PETER'S SELF-DEFENSE AT JERUSALEM (11:1-18)

What has happened in Caesarea is not a minor issue of local interest only; it affects the foundations of the self-understanding of Jewish-Christian identity. This is of such vital importance for Luke's theological concept that the story has to be retold. The Jerusalem church authorities function as critical readers. They formulate the key objection: how can a Jew, even a Jew who believes in Christ, consort with Gentiles the way Peter has done and eat with them (11:3; see above the comments about 10:28)? Peter has violated a central requirement of Torah. This has to be put under scrutiny, especially since Peter has always emphasized his strong adherence to Jewish faith and customs. Peter is the first to be accused of apostasy by his fellow church leaders! It will not be easy to defend himself.

Just like Paul's own reports about his conversion in Acts 22 and 26, this is an opportunity to hear from Peter himself what has happened. Of course he begins with his own vision. He retells it basically the way it's been narrated before in 10:9-16, with two exceptions. One is the omission of the detail that he was hungry when he experienced his vision. Second, in 10:14 he refers to not having *eaten* anything that is common or unclean, but he uses a more general term in 11:8 when he says that nothing common or unclean has ever *entered his mouth* (cf. Mark 7:18-19). Of course this includes food, but in generalizing the issue Peter emphasizes his firm stance on Jewish faith and practice as such.

Another striking feature of Peter's account is that Cornelius is not mentioned even once by name. This underlines the idea that what happened in Caesarea was not a local, one-time incident; rather, it is of great importance for the future course of all Christian communities. It affects their self-understanding. In welcoming Peter at his house in Caesarea, Cornelius himself is already aware of the reason for this divine matching. It's about salvation, for Peter is to speak "words" (Greek: *rhemata*, which takes on the meaning of "holy words") to him by which he and all his household "will be saved" (Acts 11:14). What had seemed to both Cornelius and Peter to be a riddle here appears to have been clear from the beginning. The gospel proclamation is about salvation and the call to repent and receive forgiveness of sins, to be baptized, and thus to share in the hope for resurrection (cf. Peter's Pentecost sermon in Acts 2). This gospel news has now been extended to the God-fearing Gentile world, an event that had already been announced and declared (Luke 2:29-32; 24:47).

Yet another difference is to be observed in Peter's telling of his encounter with Cornelius. Here he mentions that from the beginning of his sermon the Holy Spirit had been poured out (Acts 11:15). From the outset, this divine presence makes Peter appear to be more in control of the situation. Peter's sermon to Cornelius is authorized by God's Holy Spirit. Who then can oppose this divine approval and sanctification? The answer to this rhetorical question is clear: Nobody! Even the Jerusalem church authorities are convinced now; they are "silenced" (v. 18), which means that all their objections are repudiated as unwarranted. They consent—even more, they rejoice and glorify God: "So God has granted repentance unto life to the Gentiles as well."

The last step in God's salvific plan has been successfully accomplished. This means that in Luke-Acts all basic theological issues have been dealt with and solved. What follows will be of minor theological importance. This may sound strange, for now Paul will be the key narrative figure, but he will not have to solve any important theological problems. This is for a good reason, for Luke stresses that Paul is a loyal follower of what has been established by Peter and the Jerusalem church. The major breakthrough to the God-fearing Gentiles, their inclusion in the community, has been accomplished through Peter, who becomes the first missionary to the Gentiles. This is Luke's view and is not to be harmonized with Paul's own account in Galatians 1 and 2 in which he stresses that he has been entrusted with the gospel to the Gentiles, while Peter and the other Jerusalem apostles are to preach the gospel to Jews. If Peter had been the first to inaugurate the mission to Gentiles, Paul definitely would have had to mention it, especially in such a critical situation as his writing to the Galatians. But he does not, which is strong evidence that Luke's account of Peter's meeting with Cornelius is not historical, at least not historical in the sense that this was the first incident in a Gentile-Christian mission. Barnabas and Paul and the Antioch church were likely the first to establish such a mission.

AN AFTERTHOUGHT:
THE OPEN WOUND OF JEWISH-GENTILE
RELATIONSHIPS

The fact that in Luke's narrative Peter takes on the responsibility of being the first to help inaugurate the mission to the Gentiles demonstrates that the inclusion of the Gentiles without the Torah was a highly controversial issue that threatened the unity of the early church. Was the community to stay within the boundaries of Judaism or was it to leave and become a Gentile religion with Jewish roots and background? This question was the key issue, and by opting for the latter the Christian church became highly successful in the Roman Empire and eventually took over. But one negative side effect was that Judaism has been seen as inferior to Christianity throughout the ages, from the first hostile anti-Jewish remarks in the NT (to name but one: John 8:44), to the polemical anti-Jewish writings of the church fathers, to the persecutions of Jews during the crusades in the Middle Ages, to the horrors of the *Shoah* in our own time. All that Christians ought not to be was placed onto Jews; see, for example, the portrayal of the Pharisees in Matthew 23 or the Jews in general in the Gospel of John. Luke-Acts is no exception to this generalization (see chapter 5 on Paul's conversion and the Exegetical Introduction). It is important to stress that the narrative analysis of Acts 10:1-11:18 methodologically has to retell and make visible Luke's story. But how to apply this narrative to us Christians nowadays is a different matter. We have to keep in mind that what is said positively about those of us who are from among the Gentiles—that we as God-fearers have gained access to the God of Israel through Jesus Christ—also has a negative side in that it devalues the basis of Torah-believing Jews. In light of Christ, the Torah is given only a second position after him. These two models of God's salvation are rooted in the same promise and holy book, yet are exclusive of each other and cannot be harmonized. Christians must be aware that their view of Judaism is an ideological view based on the NT writings, which represent first-century reflections about a deep conflict among Jews who believe in Christ concerning how to view Gentiles. Are they to be included without circumcision or not? The rejection of circumcision marks the break from Judaism, even though Luke and even more so Paul claim that circumcision is still in accordance with Jewish faith and practice. On this issue Jews and Christians will most likely never agree. It remains unresolved, an open wound. For Jews to give up on Torah would mean no less than giving up on their identity! Christians should keep this in mind when they read and interpret the NT.

HOMILETIC POSSIBILITIES FOR DIVINE MATCHING: THE BREAKTHROUGH OF THE GOSPEL INTO THE GENTILE WORLD *OR* THE CONVERSION OF PETER

Once again, the exegesis of this text invites us to reflect homiletically not only on the success of the gospel for the Gentiles, but also on the rejection it meets among Jews. Luke's answer is to attribute this rejection to God's hardening of their hearts. What if, however, the preaching of the gospel in light of this text gave us an opportunity to reopen Luke's original theological question? In this way, perhaps we can tend to the "open wound" that our exegete describes. Perhaps we can begin to heal that which is at the heart of the anti-Judaism of our text and tend to the persistent grief that gnaws at contemporary Christianity, as well.

Introduction
Good news is bad news.

With the introduction we frame the problem. The good news of Cornelius's acceptance opens up a series of problems for Peter and the leaders of the church in Jerusalem. We might set it up this way:

There's an old routine from the movies. A group of employees has drawn lots and the loser's job is to go tell some higher-up something that's difficult to say. How do they put it? "Well, boss," they hem and haw, "there's good news and there's bad news. Which do you want?" With Cornelius and Peter the old routine gets an even older twist. Cornelius hears that God has accepted him and his prayers. Call it good news. Peter, however, before hearing the report, would not have believed that God had accepted a Gentile. Call it bad news. So what do you do with messengers approaching? What do you do when good news is bad news?

Scene 1
Peter would have wanted to make a Gentile like
Cornelius fit into the way things were.

Preachers should have a fairly easy time with this scene. Peter here is the representative authority. It is his job to make things "fit." The problem is, this Cornelius guy, whose representatives are on their way to meet him, doesn't seem to fit the prescribed pattern. Preachers need only describe the scene about to unfold and contemporize it with our own ecclesiastical analogues. They are legion.

> Peter's solution is to make the Corneliuses of this world fit the mold. He knows all the old ecclesiastical formulae. Doubtless his favorite one is the church's version of the last seven last words of Christ: "We've never done it that way before." At any rate, before Peter even hears the news, he would be sure in his heart. His response would be simple. He would assume that Cornelius or any other Gentile must be instructed on the proper order of things: first circumcision, then baptism.

Scene 2
Before Cornelius's messengers show up, the Spirit
surprises Peter with a vision.

With this scene, the complication deepens. Just when Peter thinks all such matters have been settled, the Spirit interrupts with a troubling vision and a direct order. The vision comes before Cornelius's news even arrives: "Slaughter and eat." As if to drive the point home, the instruction becomes more explicit as Peter resists: "What God has cleansed, you must not call common." Here preachers may want to focus on congregations' struggles with competing revelations as a way of identifying with Peter's dilemma. The choices presenting themselves are not altogether obvious. Peter, once certain, is now troubled—by the Spirit. Perhaps Peter should have read a little Henri Nouwen, whose wise friend notes that "my interruptions [are] my work."[9] And so they are—look at Peter, for whom all seemed settled until the Spirit interrupted him with a vision.

Scene 3
With the arrival of the news, suddenly Peter
gets the picture: God is impartial.

Here preachers can try to help congregations envision how a new way of looking at things emerges. One might try to draw an analogy from our day.

> Scientific revolutions tend to work this way. At first, they start with disparate pieces of evidence that don't fit the dominant paradigm. After a while, the evidence adds up and begins pointing to a competing way of looking at the world. Over time, a new scientific paradigm is assembled and its explanatory power becomes the new dominant worldview. Whether it's a flat earth, evolutionary ancestry, or the debate over homosexuality—sometimes things change because another truth dawns on us. Well, the same kind of thing seems to happen to Peter. His worldview was settled before: circumcision, then baptism. But then the new evidence begins to gnaw at the edges of his known world: visions of unclean food, divine commands from the Spirit to listen to a Gentile like Cornelius, and then Cornelius's own report of his vision. The evidence at this point overwhelms Peter: "Truly I realize now that God shows no partiality. . . ." And with these words, a worldview begins to crumble and a new world starts taking shape. Seeing the Spirit among them, Peter now can't help but baptize.

Scene 4
So where does that leave us? With an appealing gospel!

This is a crucial moment for preachers wishing to get at the tragic underside of this text. From here we move out of the narrative
order of the plot to consider the theological significance of the
choices made. Here preachers will want to survey how this broad
swath of inclusion, represented by the welcoming of the Gentiles,
has revolutionized Christian faith. In breaking down Torah restric-
tions, Christianity hit the big time. For communities who felt marginalized, this break was decisive. Again and again in our history,
we have come to terms with increasingly broader visions of God's
love for humanity. Sure, the church has more often than not resisted
change and taken steps away from inclusion. Nonetheless, the
theo-logic of its own ethnic boundary crossing in the early church
has been an impetus for transformation that seems inherent to
Christian faith. Every time we set up a new barrier to divine grace,
the Spirit reminds us, as it did Peter, of God's absolute freedom to
love. This has been our appeal as Christianity has become a worldwide phenomenon.

Scene 5
The change has also left us with a wound: a broken relationship with God's people, Israel.

The problem here is palpable. We Christians have tended to set
up Jews as a foil in the way we relate this gospel of crossing boundaries. If the issue is inclusion, we paint "the Jews" as exclusive and
narrow-minded. If the issue is ethnic identity, we portray "the
Jews" as primitively ethnocentric. If the issue is the Law versus
freedom, we turn "the Jews" into punctilious legalists. None of this
squares with the living reality of Judaism. Nonetheless, it persists
in our preaching and teaching, in part because we assume that our
freedom, liberation, and inclusion requires someone else's legalism,
bondage, and exclusivity as a foil. In the process, we have failed to
recognize our Jewish brothers and sisters for who they really are.

Conclusion

So what do you know? Perhaps our problem goes to the core of the gospel news itself. Good news is bad news is good news. We Christians have tried to justify ourselves by turning the Jews into what they are not. Yet if we remember our gospel, we may just be converted ourselves. According to the gospel, we need no longer justify ourselves or anyone else—especially the Jews. Peter's choice lies open to us this day as well. Can we move beyond the grief of choosing between the Spirit and the scriptures as Peter did? Only, people of God, only by God's own gospel of grace for us *and* for our Jewish brothers and sisters.

CONCLUSION

Preaching with Our Little Hero Paul in Big Athens

Acts 17:22-31

Lectionary: Year A, Sixth Sunday of Easter

We now move beyond finding a preachable edge to a difficult lectionary text in Luke-Acts. Indeed, following Paul, reluctant as he is to preach the gospel to Gentiles, perhaps we can find a new place to stand, as well. Why? As we have seen all the way through, the stakes are enormous. We, like Paul, must discern the meaning of the gospel for our times with a Gospel (Luke, along with Acts) whose legacy is troubling. What will we do?

Here we begin to bump into one of the classic problems associated with Luke-Acts. Many have claimed that Luke's two-part work represents the ultimate "success" theology of the NT. The great NT scholar Ernst Käsemann argued that Luke-Acts embodies a "theology of glory," in stark contrast to the superior "theology of the cross" in Paul's epistles. He judged the author of Luke-Acts to be theologically deficient because of the way he portrayed the early church: big numbers, big healings—one big glorious deal. In truth, his accusation had some weight. Luke's universal reach is stunningly success-oriented: "You will be my witnesses in Jerusalem, in all Judea and Samaria, and to the ends of the earth" (Acts 1:8). Luke clearly has worldwide aspirations and a glorious gospel in view.

Nonetheless, we have also seen in our survey of some sample lectionary texts in Luke-Acts that the epithet "theology of glory" is less than adequate. There is surrounding this epic story a kind of tragic failure. Luke's Jesus is rejected in his hometown, his own disciples require coaching to recognize him on the road to Emmaus, and Acts' final protagonist (Paul) keeps resisting his calling in a seemingly futile attempt to appeal to the Jews of the Mediterranean world. All is not glorious in this so-called theology of glory.

Yet perhaps this underside of failure and tragedy is precisely the point where we can begin to reenvision our ministry of preaching. If the truth be told, we've had it good. Those of us who are mainline Protestants may well even remember the days when the leaders of churches were paraded through the White House like visiting dignitaries. Yet now, apart from the occasional photo-op, we have been relegated to the margins with shrinking membership rolls, scared institutions, and languishing leadership. Now more than ever, the old success gospel of numbers and pride of influence is bumping into the tragic character of our day-to-day church realities. Perhaps we, like Paul, are in a unique position to come to terms with the troubling legacy of both Luke-Acts and our own history, where our dreams of success have been shattered on the hard realities of the now-receding twentieth century: the *deus ex machina* determinism of neoconservative global capitalism, the disestablishment of our increasingly fragmented churches, and of course, the troubling moral legacy of Christian complicity in the Holocaust.

Therefore, let us now listen in on Paul's sermon in Acts 17:22-31 in its context. He must find a way to preach the gospel to one of the great intellectual centers of the empire, Athens. As we listen to his sermon, perhaps we can discover a preaching stance for an almost exclusively Gentile church that is asking questions about the gospel all over again.

Text

[16]While Paul was waiting for them in Athens, his spirit within him was angered, as he saw the city full of idols. [17]So he argued in

the synagogue with the Jews and the God-fearing Gentiles; and every day in the public square with those who chanced to be there. ¹⁸Some of the Epicurean and Stoic philosophers met with him; and some of them would ask, "What would this seed picker be trying to tell us?" Others would say, "He seems to be lobbying for foreign deities," because he was preaching Jesus and the resurrection. ¹⁹So they took him and led him to the Areopagus, saying, "May we know what this new teaching is that is being presented by you? ²⁰For you are bringing up subjects foreign to our ears; we therefore want to know what this is all about." ²¹Now all the Athenians as well as the foreigners residing with them used to spend their time in nothing else but telling or hearing something new.

²²So Paul, standing in the middle of the Areopagus, said: "People of Athens, I see that in every respect you are very religious. ²³For as I passed along, and looked carefully at the objects of your worship, I even came upon an altar with the inscription "To a God Unknown." Now what you thus worship unknowingly, this I proclaim to you. ²⁴The God who made the world and all that is in it, this being the Lord of heaven and earth, does not live in temples made by human hands. ²⁵Nor is it as if he lacks anything or is served by human hands. It is rather he who gives everyone life and breath and everything else. ²⁶From one people he made all the human race dwell on the face of the whole earth. He it is who has fixed the dates of their epochs and boundaries of their habitation, ²⁷so that they might seek God and perhaps even grope for him and find him, even though he is not far from each one of us. ²⁸For in him we live and move and have our being. As some of your poets have put it: "For we are indeed his offspring." ²⁹Being then God's offspring, we ought not to think that Deity is something like a statue of gold, of silver, or of stone, a work of human art and conception. ³⁰God overlooked the times of ignorance, but now he commands all people everywhere to repent, ³¹because he has set a day on which he is going to judge the world in righteousness through a man whom he has appointed, and whom he has endorsed before all by raising him from the dead."

³²Now when they heard of the resurrection of the dead, some of them sneered, but others said: "We will hear you about this matter again some other time." ³³At that point Paul left them. ³⁴A few of

them, however, did join him and became believers; among them were Dionysius, a member of the Areopagus, and a woman named Damaris, and some others. (Author's translation)

ANALYSIS

"And some others"—is this what you would call success? Hardly. Remember how Luke loves big numbers? Literally thousands of Jews join Peter's Christian party and are baptized as a result of his harsh Pentecost sermon: first three thousand (Acts 2:41), and then five thousand (Acts 4:4), with James declaring that "many thousands" of Jews had come to faith in Christ (Acts 21:20). What a success story—had there not been opposition from other Jews. Therefore, the number of those who are convinced by Paul's preaching in Athens is striking. There are so few that Luke can mention them by their names: one man and one woman, a certain Dionysius and Damaris—and, of course, a few others. Was nothing more to be expected? This Paul seems to be more successful among Jews, in spite of all the turmoil and tribulations they have caused him. Remember that the gospel is addressed not only to Israel but also to the entire world. Paul is having a hard time accepting his own call as outlined by the Lord, namely, to proclaim Christ Jesus primarily to Gentiles; Jews come only second in this missionary scheme (Acts 9:15). Yet Paul still follows the same pattern when entering a new city: he always marches straight into a synagogue first, wherever there is one. This Paul is having a hard time learning his lesson. How must he feel after such a failure in Athens? Jews are giving him a hard time, and after he tries preaching the gospel among pagan Gentiles, those results are not encouraging, either. Well, there is a kind of consolation: at least he doesn't have to suffer physical violence—it's only a verbal put-down. But it must hurt. Wherever Paul goes, he either gets kicked out of the city or persecuted and imprisoned or, when he actually tries to reach out to a Gentile audience, they try to worship him as a god (as in Lystra) or he is ridiculed (as in Athens). Whatever he tries, he seems to be on the wrong side of life.

Paul's life and mission is not a success story. Can you see the apologetic side of this Lukan portrayal? We learn about a Paul who is very much down-to-earth: sad and funny to watch and to follow. He can so bore his audience with his long sermons that some young guy, probably a confirmand or catechumen, falls out of the window (Acts 20:7-9). Who can "survive" a sermon that lasts from supper until midnight? Paul then can preach so boldly and impressively that even King Agrippa is almost tempted to become a Christian—but ironically, since he appealed to Caesar, he has to go to Rome (Acts 26:28-32).

Most commentators have focused on the supposed importance of Paul's speech at the Areopagus in Athens. Hardly anybody seems to fully recognize the Jewishness of the speech. In his recent commentary, Fitzmyer calls it "one of the highlights of Acts," it being "the second most important Pauline speech in Acts."[1] Despite noting that "its message is mainly theological, not christological," he does not take the next step and compare it to other speeches addressed to Gentiles.[2] The Lukan Paul behaves in an utterly Jewish manner insofar as the first step for converting pagan Gentiles to Christianity is to make them behave in the manner of God-fearers like Cornelius. Still, the Lukan Paul fails.

Instead of being concerned only with the speech itself, one should also pay attention to its narrative framework. There is some important information to be discerned that gives the sermon a somewhat different perspective and meaning. Some scholars have viewed this speech as the earliest and thus most important Christian attempt to engage with Greco-Roman philosophy, but it also reveals some insights into the futility of preaching. The ironic elements outweigh the philosophical depths of this speech. It is more a presentation of our little hero Paul in big Athens than an impressive philosophical discourse about the truth of Christianity.

View it from the perspective of Luke's audience: our hero Paul has finally made it to Athens, which, though it isn't Rome, still has a special aura of culture and knowledge. Thus, it makes sense for Paul to stop at Athens on the way to Corinth, particularly since he has to wait for his colleagues Silas and Timothy (Acts 17:16). So what else is there to do besides going around to have a look at the city? But first Paul has to stop by the local synagogue. After all, he is a Jew! Here he becomes upset with what he sees: the city is full of handmade idols. This makes him, the devout Jew who believes in Christ, furious and he begins to argue with everyone he happens to bump into. Some philosophers of the Epicurean and Stoic schools hear him and ask, "What does this seed picker say?"—indicating that to them he sounds like one who incorporates bits of thought from different philosophical schools, just like a bird who picks seed. But what is his strange philosophy all about? Is he perhaps speaking about two new gods, a male and a female one? A certain Jesus and a female goddess called "Resurrection" (the Greek noun *anastasis* is feminine)? They haven't heard of either one of them.

Athenians were known worldwide for their curiosity and chattiness, and they invite him to the Areopagus. No special honor is involved in this; anybody could go there and listen to all kinds of speeches, good ones as well as rhetorically poor ones. Think of it more like Speaker's Corner at London's Hyde Park. This is the kind of atmosphere we have to imagine when trying to grasp the situation Paul has gotten himself into. Remember, he is still full of anger. So listen to what our little hero has to say.

He starts out excellently! Instead of attacking them and confronting them with their blasphemous idolatry, he fishes for compliments by acknowledging their religious goodwill (v. 22). But goodwill does not always mean good choices. So in pointing out an altar dedicated to an unknown god, he begins to talk about the God of Israel who, although invisible, is nonetheless the true maker of heaven and earth and of all creation. This one and only true God is the sole source of all of humanity, and thus is to be recognized by human insight (cf. Rom. 1:20-21). In emphasizing the unity of all humankind, Paul demonstrates his knowledge by quoting from popular Greek philosophy, which stressed the same point (Acts 17:28). However, the true God (of Israel) is not to be found in handmade statues, but was made visible in "a man whom he has appointed, and whom he has endorsed before all by raising him from the dead" (v. 31). The supposedly unknown God has taken on a human face in Jesus and his resurrection. Interestingly enough, Jesus is mentioned by name in this speech, but it is also striking that out of all the events of Jesus' life, only his resurrection is mentioned. This reminds us of Peter's first Pentecost speech, which also focused on the resurrection and the exaltation of Christ to the right hand of God (Acts 2:32). The divine presence of Christ in God's Holy Spirit constituted the call for repentance for the Jews (2:38) just as it now does for the pagan Gentiles (17:30). But whereas the Jews were willing to repent and even to accept responsibility for an unjustified participation in a just cause ("Jesus whom you crucified" Acts 2:36), the Athenians remain ignorant. They start to mock Paul (v. 19), as if to say, "We were curious about what you had to say, and maybe at times it even appeared to sound quite interesting, but this now is going too far. It's simply ridiculous." Those who are more polite tell him that they might give him a second chance if it ever comes up (v. 32), while others are more frank and just leave laughing. Poor Paul! Nice try, but no success. What success he does have can practically be counted on one hand: two out of an audience of maybe a few hundred who listened to him—and some others—are won for the Christian cause.

EPILOGUE FOR PREACHERS WHO
FOLLOW THE LUKAN PAUL

What do we do with a Paul like this—one who seems to be something of a failure? Strange as it may sound, perhaps we can count him as a homiletical friend.

To be sure, we can't embrace the solution that the Lukan Paul comes to. After all his disappointments and failures in preaching to the Jews, Paul in Acts 28:25-28 quotes Isaiah's prophecy to his Jewish listeners. The upshot of the quote is that their refusal of the gospel is viewed as a result of their hardness of heart, one that is, as our exegete notes, divinely willed.[3] This is a theological solution that is no longer tenable for us in a post-Holocaust context.

Yet the grief over the failure that gave Luke's narrated theology birth may just offer us an opportunity to revisit the issue. We, after all, share the legacy of that grief. Certainly, most of us do not distribute tracts at the local synagogue. Yet the dark underside of our universalistic impulses (whether it is to evangelize the world or to bring in the reign of God in global peace and justice) is that the Jewish people did not see the gospel the same way our forebears in faith did. Lest we think that, since we don't spend nights tossing and turning over whether Jews convert to Christianity, the whole issue is now passé, we must let ourselves be reminded of the unspeakable violence that happened to the Jewish people at largely Christian hands. In other words, the legacy of Luke's anti-Judaism is our anti-Semitism—and anti-Semitism *is* a Christian problem. We, apparently, need to work through our unresolved Christian grief so that it doesn't surprise us again, reemerging hydralike in some new twenty-first-century guise.

However, another important point of contact between us and the grieving, Lukan Paul lies in the repeated failure of his preaching. We, of late, find ourselves failing, too—not only with "those Jews," but also with Gentiles like us, as well. Like the Lukan Paul, we may be tempted to assign blame, whether to the culture or to our own lack of faith in the God who rewards faith with success. It might be better, however, to acknowledge failure as an invitation to think more deeply about preaching as it relates to the mystery of God. How can we feel called to preach, gifted to preach, and still experience the failure of the mainline church to grow or to affect political and economic systems in light of God's kingdom? Only if our failure and Paul's failure are more than they seem. What if, for example, they participate in some deeper sense in a divine mystery?

What mystery? The mystery of Jesus' own death. At the cross, there is nothing that says we must interpret failure as a divine rejection of us or anyone else. Moreover, we should not forget that he also *remained* dead—for three days. This was no "seeming" death. As if to help us get the point, God even drew it out for three days. Three days meant Jesus was *really* dead.

Only then is it possible to talk about resurrection. And when we do, let us remember that the risen one still bore and bears the marks of his failure. They didn't disappear. Now we can rejoice that the one who bears those marks sits at God's right hand in the eternity of heaven. This is all to say that failure—even ours and even Paul's—does not place us outside of the divine mystery, but right in the middle of it.

Perhaps once we do this, we will finally be ready for true inter-faith dialogue. As admitted failures, we need no longer be troubled that any Jewish rejection of the gospel, past or present, will somehow disclose our shame. No, we will have already embraced it in the fellowship of our weak, failed preaching. And maybe, just maybe, on that day we will be able to dialogue because we see ourselves and the Jewish people with new vision: as God's beloved peoples.

NOTES

PREFACE FOR PREACHERS

1. Shelley Cochran, for example, identifies several problems and pitfalls associated with the "Lukan Prominence" that the church year, and derivatively the Revised Common Lectionary, presupposes (*The Pastor's Underground Guide to the Revised Common Lectionary: Year B* [St. Louis: Chalice, 1996], pp. 26-28).

2. Following convention, I refer to Luke as the author of Luke-Acts. I am fully aware of the critical difficulties attending the attribution of authorship here and the flawed gender assumptions they embody. "Sinning boldly," I use the name "Luke" as shorthand for the author of the two-part work. For a more detailed critical assessment of the issues of authorship and the relation of Luke and Acts, see the "Exegetical Introduction to Luke-Acts" that follows.

3. To be sure, this interpretation of Acts 28:25-28 is controversial (cf. Robert Brawley, *Luke-Acts and the Jews: Conflict, Apology, and Conciliation* [Atlanta: Scholars Press, 1987]). The crucial question is what the word *epachunthe* ("have grown dull") means in verse 27. How do we interpret the passive? Our exegete, Günter Wasserberg, argues convincingly that it must be understood as a *passivum divinum*, which means that God stands behind the hardening of the hearts of those Jews who reject the gospel of Christ. A related question is the prominent place of the Isaiah quotation at the end of Acts. The final scene marks the end not only of the pericope but also of the whole narrative and thus leaves a lasting impression on its readers. Thus, the Lukan Paul's proclamation to the Jews of Rome has to be seen as general in scope, not just local. For further information, see Günter's "Exegetical Introduction to Luke-Acts" that follows and a more

detailed treatment in his book *Aus Israels Mitte-Heil für die Welt: Eine narrativ-exegetische Studie zur Theologie des Lukas* (Berlin: Walter de Gruyter, 1998), pp. 108-9.

4. "Points" refers to a logical and categorical mode of structuring sermons, either deductively or inductively. Either the sermon starts from a point, and moving deductively from it, proves it by appealing to experience; or the sermon starts with experience, and moving inductively through it, arrives at a final, single point as a kind of homiletical "aha!" moment. "Moves" refers to modes of sermon development that try to shape preaching in the form of consciousness. David G. Buttrick (*Homiletic: Moves and Structures* [Philadelphia: Fortress Press, 1987]) and Henry Mitchell (*Celebration and Experience in Preaching* [Nashville: Abingdon Press, 1990]) are perhaps its chief representatives. Narrated stock "plots" refers to the work of many narrative preachers and homileticians. However, the dean of this school of homiletical thought is Eugene Lowry. In his earlier work, Lowry posited five narrated stock plot elements (see *The Homiletical Plot* [Atlanta: John Knox, 1980], 25). In a more recent work, Lowry seems to think that the typical narrative plot needs only the four elements: discrepancy, complication, reversal, and resolution (*The Sermon: Dancing the Edge of Mystery* [Nashville: Abingdon Press, 1997], p. 23).

5. For a fascinating history of the persistence of such attitudes in Christian preaching, see Clark M. Williamson and Ronald J. Allen, *Interpreting Difficult Texts: Anti-Judaism and Christian Preaching* (Philadelphia: Trinity, 1989), pp. 9-27.

EXEGETICAL INTRODUCTION TO LUKE-ACTS

1. Richard I. Pervo and Mikeal C. Parsons, *Rethinking the Unity of Luke and Acts* (Minneapolis: Augsburg Fortress, 1993).

2. The authors prefer the designation Hebrew Bible (abbreviated HB from here onward) to Old Testament (OT) as a way of acknowledging its ongoing integrity and validity.

1. THE PRESENTATION OF JESUS AT THE TEMPLE (LUKE 2:22-40)

1. Ernst Käsemann, *Essays on New Testament Themes*, trans. W. J. Montague (London: SCM Press Ltd., 1964), p. 92.

2. Jacob Jervell, "The Circumcised Messiah" in *The Unknown Paul: Essays on Luke-Acts and Early Christian History* (Minneapolis: Augsburg Publishing House, 1984).

3. For example, Raymond E. Brown, *The Birth of the Messiah* (Garden City, N.Y.: Doubleday, 1977), p. 241.

2. PROCLAMATION AND CONFRONTATION AT NAZARETH (LUKE 4:14-30)

1. Alfred Henry Leaney, *A Commentary on the Gospel According to St. Luke, Second Edition* (London: A. & C. Black, 1966), p. 52.

3. HOPE FOR RESURRECTION: A LEARNING EXPERIENCE (LUKE 24:13-49)

1. Jacob Jervell, "The Circumcised Messiah" in *The Unknown Paul: Essays on Luke-Acts and Early Christian History* (Minneapolis: Augsburg Publishing House, 1984).

2. Robert C. Tannehill, *The Narrative Unity of Luke-Acts, Vol. 2: The Acts of the Apostles* (Minneapolis: Fortress Press, 1990), p. 345.

3. Joseph A. Fitzmyer, *The Gospel According to Luke (X-XXIV)* (The Anchor Bible, Vol. 28a; Garden City, N.Y.: Doubleday, 1985), p. 1565.

4. For a thorough discussion of the problem of Luke's soteriology, see Joseph A. Fitzmyer, *The Gospel According to Luke (I-IX)* (The Anchor Bible, Vol. 28; New York: Doubleday, 1981), pp. 219-23.

5. Fred B. Craddock, *As One Without Authority* (Nashville: Abingdon Press, 1971), p. 78.

6. This insight about returning to proclaim in the darkness is not my own. This was pointed out to me by some pastoral interns of the Evangelical Lutheran Church of Peru (ILEP) and by a lay Bible study group at Luz Divina, a small Peruvian Lutheran congregation in one of the "Young Cities" on the edge of Lima. I was in Peru in April 1999 to help teach preaching to future pastors of the newly indigenized Lutheran church there. Oddly enough, it was they who taught me. Perhaps God still does open eyes and hearts far away from home—even mine.

4. PENTECOST: A JEWISH SPRING OF THE CHURCH (ACTS 2:1-21; 2:14-41; 2:42-47)

1. For a treatment of the issue in Romans, see Günter Wasserberg, "Romans 9–11 and Jewish-Christian Dialogue: Prospects and Provisos" in *Reading Israel in Romans: Legitimacy and Plausibility of Divergent Interpretations,* eds. Cristina Grenholm and Daniel Patte (Harrisburg, Pa.: Trinity, 2000), pp. 174-86.

2. Robert C. Tannehill, *The Narrative Unity of Luke-Acts, Vol. 2: The Acts of the Apostles* (Minneapolis: Fortress Press, 1990), p. 28.

3. Hans Conzelmann, *Acts of the Apostles,* trans. James Limburg, A. Thomas Kraabel, and Donald H. Juel (Philadelphia: Fortress Press, 1987), p. 19.

4. Peter probably missed the homiletics class on how to win an audience, or he was too hotheaded to have paid enough attention to what the teachers said. At any rate, how do we as preachers feel about texts that make us uneasy? Maybe this is not a good example to test a preacher's integrity and courage.

5. Krister Stendahl, *Paul Among Jews and Gentiles* (Philadelphia: Fortress Press, 1976), p. 37.

5. THE PERSECUTED PERSECUTOR: THE CONVERSION OF PAUL (ACTS 9:1-31)

1. Cf. Jürgen Becker, *Paul: Apostle to the Gentiles,* trans. O. C. Dean (Louisville: Westminster John Knox, 1996).

2. For example, Günter Klein, *Die zwölf Apostel: Ursprung und Gehalt einer Idee* (FRLANT 77; Göttingen: Vandenhoeck & Ruprecht, 1961), p. 146.

3. Daniel Marguerat, "Saul's Conversion (Acts 9, 22, 26) and the Multiplication of Narrative in Acts" in *Luke's Literary Achievement: Collected Essays,* ed. C. M. Tuckett (JSNTS 116; Sheffield: Sheffield Academic Press, 1995), p. 141.

4. Robert C. Tannehill, *The Narrative Unity of Luke-Acts, Vol. 2: The Acts of the Apostles* (Minneapolis: Fortress Press, 1990), p. 116.

5. Ernst Käsemann, *Essays on New Testament Themes,* trans. W. J. Montague (London: SCM Press Ltd., 1964), p. 92.

6. DIVINE MATCHING: THE BREAKTHROUGH OF THE GOSPEL INTO THE GENTILE WORLD *OR* THE CONVERSION OF PETER (ACTS 10:1–11:18)

1. Robert C. Tannehill, *The Narrative Unity of Luke-Acts, Vol. 2: The Acts of the Apostles* (Minneapolis: Fortress Press, 1990), p. 109.

2. Joseph A. Fitzmyer, *The Acts of the Apostles* (The Anchor Bible, Vol. 31; New York: Doubleday, 1998), p. 446.

3. Cf. Klaus Wengst, *Pax Romana: and the peace of Jesus Christ* (Philadelphia: Fortress Press, 1987); Günter Wasserberg, *Aus Israels Mitte-Heil für die Welt: Eine narrativ-exegetische Studie zur Theologie des Lukas* (Berlin: Walter de Gruyter, 1998), pp. 60-62, 73-74.

4. Whether the term "God-fearer" technically refers to a group by this name or not (see Wasserberg, *Aus Israels Mitte*, pp. 44-67), it has no direct implications for a narrative approach.

5. Fitzmyer, *Acts of the Apostles*, p. 451.

6. See Bruce J. Malina, *The New Testament World: Insights from Cultural Anthropology* (Atlanta: John Knox Press, 1981), p. 135.

7. Philip F. Esler, *Community and Gospel in Luke-Acts: The Social and Political Motivations of Lucan Theology* (Cambridge: Cambridge University Press, 1987), p. 84.

8. See Wasserberg, *Aus Israels Mitte*, pp. 297-303.

9. Henri J. M. Nouwen, *Out of Solitude: Three Meditations on the Christian Life* (Notre Dame, Ind.: Ave Maria, 1974), p. 56.

CONCLUSION: PREACHING WITH OUR LITTLE HERO PAUL IN BIG ATHENS (ACTS 17:22-31)

1. Joseph A. Fitzmyer, *The Acts of the Apostles* (The Anchor Bible, Vol. 31; New York: Doubleday, 1998), p. 601.

2. Ibid.

3. Günter Wasserberg, *Aus Israels Mitte-Heil für die Welt: Eine narrativ-exegetische Studie zur Theologie des Lukas* (Berlin: Walter de Gruyter, 1998), pp. 108-9.

APPENDIX

Resources for Narrative Exegesis and Preaching on Luke-Acts

Commentaries and Biblical Resources

Brawley, Robert L. *Luke-Acts and the Jews: Conflict, Apology, and Conciliation*. Atlanta: Scholars Press, 1987.
Brawley's work represents a new phase of scholarship in Luke-Acts. Rather than assume that the work is directed only to Gentiles, he views Luke-Acts as an attempt to tie an emergent Gentile Christianity to Judaism.

Fitzmyer, Joseph A. *The Gospel According to Luke* (2 vols.). Garden City, N.Y.: Doubleday, 1985.

———. *The Acts of the Apostles*. New York: Doubleday, 1998.
Again, though not literary or narrative in perspective, these commentaries are encyclopedic relative to historical issues in and behind the text of Luke.

Kingsbury, Jack. *Conflict in Luke*. Minneapolis: Fortress Press, 1991.
Kingsbury applies narrative criticism to the Gospel by focusing on conflict as the key to Luke's plot.

O'Day, Gail R. "Acts" in *The Women's Bible Commentary*. Eds. Carol A. Newsom and Sharon E. Ringe. Louisville: Westminster John Knox, 1992.
O'Day sees potential in using the writer's interest in erasing ethnic boundary lines between clean and unclean as a model for better gender relations.

Reimer, Ivoni Richter. *Women in the Acts of the Apostles: A Feminist Liberation Perspective*. Trans. Linda M. Maloney. Minneapolis: Augsburg Fortress, 1995.

Reimer, a Brazilian scholar, writes self-consciously from a feminist liberation-theological perspective and focuses on understanding frequently neglected female characters in Acts.

Ringe, Sharon H. *Luke.* Louisville: Westminster John Knox, 1995.
Ringe's commentary does a great job of taking into account the social and historical context of the Gospel even while asking questions of what the text means for us today.

Schaberg, Jane. "Luke" in *The Women's Bible Commentary.* Eds. Carol A. Newsom and Sharon E. Ringe. Louisville: Westminster John Knox, 1992.
Schaberg cautions readers to be careful about assuming that Luke is enlightened in his depiction of women. Luke often portrays female characters in a way that legitimates male dominance.

Tannehill, Robert C. *Luke* (Abingdon New Testament Commentaries). Nashville: Abingdon Press, 1996.
The author offers here an accessible, narrative-critical commentary on Luke. This is an excellent choice for the preacher who wishes to ground narrative preaching in solid critical exegesis.

———. *The Narrative Unity of Luke-Acts: A Literary Interpretation* (2 vols.). Philadelphia: Fortress Press, 1986–1990.
This is a groundbreaking study for applying literary criticism to Luke-Acts as a whole. Since it is not arranged in commentary form, its value will be for the pastor who wishes to push literary criticism of the biblical text to another level.

Tyson, Joseph. *Images of Judaism in Luke-Acts.* New York: Columbia, 1992.
Tyson emphasizes the importance of the implied reader for understanding the narrative of Luke-Acts. Just as a pastor needs to understand a congregation for preaching, so a narrative critic of Luke-Acts benefits from understanding its audience.

Learning Narrative Exegesis

Patte, Daniel. *Structural Exegesis for New Testament Critics.* Minneapolis: Augsburg Fortress, 1990.
Patte's work offers unique literary insights as he applies a structuralist perspective to texts from John and Luke's Gospels.

Peterson, Norman. *Literary Criticism for New Testament Critics.* Philadelphia: Fortress Press, 1978.
Peterson features one chapter on "Narrative World and Real World in Luke-Acts."

Powell, Mark. *What Is Narrative Criticism?* Minneapolis: Fortress Press, 1990.
Powell's book is a useful introduction for those wishing to learn how to do a narrative exegesis of a biblical text.

Rhoads, David, Joanna Dewey, and Donald Michie. *Mark as Story: An Introduction to the Narrative of a Gospel* (second edition). Minneapolis: Fortress Press, 1999.
Although dealing with Mark's Gospel, this book reviews the narrative critic's tools and shows how they may be used.

Preaching and Anti-Semitism

Kee, Howard Clark and Irvin J. Borowsky, eds. *Removing Anti-Judaism from the Pulpit.* New York: Continuum, 1996.
Like most collections of essays, the chapters are uneven. Still, preachers will benefit from the variety of scholarly works and sermons it contains.

Smith, Christine M. *Preaching as Weeping, Confession, and Resistance: Radical Responses to Radical Evil.* Louisville: Westminster John Knox, 1992.
Although no single chapter is devoted to the issue of anti-Semitism, Smith's model for preaching in response to various forms of radical evil could prove useful to preachers who wish to do so.

Williamson, Clark M. and Ronald J. Allen. *Interpreting Difficult Texts: Anti-Judaism and Christian Preaching.* Philadelphia: Trinity, 1989.
Clark and Allen's book is very useful for considering the many dimensions of anti-Judaism in Christian preaching.

Preaching and Narrative

Buttrick, David G. *Homiletic: Moves and Structures.* Philadelphia: Fortress Press, 1987.
Buttrick is not a "narrative preacher." However, his thoughts on interpreting biblical narrative theologically places him in a unique position in the debate over the use of narrative theory in contemporary homiletics.

Lowry, Eugene. *The Homiletical Plot: The Sermon as Narrative Art Form.* Atlanta: John Knox, 1980.

Lowry's book, though brief, offers an excellent introduction to a plot-based understanding of narrative preaching.

Mitchell, Henry. *Celebration and Experience in Preaching.* Nashville: Abingdon Press, 1990.

Although narrative preaching is not Mitchell's sole focus, for those who wish to focus on matters of character "identification" and the possibility of "celebration" in their preaching, Mitchell also offers these and other unique insights from within African American preaching traditions in the U.S.

Riegert, Eduard. *Imaginative Shock: Preaching and Metaphor.* Burlington, Ontario: Trinity Press, 1990.

Bringing together contemporary discussions of imagination and narrative, Riegert offers wonderful insights for preaching. Riegert's emphasis on "metaphoric process" can help to deepen notions of plot reversal in narrative preaching.

Smith, Dennis E. and Michael E. Williams, eds. *The Storyteller's Companion to the Bible: Volume 12 Acts of the Apostles.* Nashville: Abingdon Press, 1999.

———. *The Storyteller's Companion to the Bible: Volume 9 Matthew-Luke.* Nashville: Abingdon Press, 2000.

These two books in the *Storyteller's* series can be of use to preachers who wish to link sensitivity to biblical narrative with contemporary storytelling in the pulpit.

Sermons

Lowry, Eugene. *How to Preach a Parable: Designs for Narrative Sermons.* Nashville: Abingdon Press, 1989.

Robinson, Wayne, ed. *Journeys Toward Narrative Preaching.* New York: Pilgrim Press, 1990.

Schlueter, Carol, ed. *The Forgotten Followers.* Winfield, British Columbia: Wood Lake Books, 1992.

Author Index

Scripture Index